Vanessa Gonçalves

I AM ENOUGH,
I AM VULNERABLE

Contents

Rather than sitting on the sidelines and hurling judgement and advice, we must dare to show up and let ourselves be seen. This is vulnerability.

Brené Brown

THE BEAUTY OF CRACKS

In December 2010, I was living my first days as Miss Venezuela.

I was overwhelmed with activities, commitments, classes. I was also beginning the grueling preparations that would take me to the Miss Universe pageant the following year. My head was a whirlwind torn between what that immense responsibility meant and the world I had pushed aside.

That same month Brené Brown's TED Talk, *The Power of Vulnerability,* had just been released.

I saw her countless times—and then I read her books and became her fan—and wanted to make my own the words and teachings of that researcher who spoke to me about shame as an emotion-mobilizing agent.

Shame, in a way, had driven a good part of my life. I was tormented by phrases like *I'm not good enough* and *I'm not adequate*; I told myself I wasn't "good enough" to deserve affection, gifts, situations, happiness, life itself—that I was not valuable enough, intelligent, independent, successful, beautiful, capable, and a thousand other things that clouded the watchful look I should have on my present and my future.

Vulnerability is a concept I've been very afraid of. I'm only coming to understand it a decade after listening to Brown for the first time.

It's about being brave enough to be imperfect. Brave enough to have compassion and accept myself. Brave enough to harbor kindness toward my many flaws. Brave enough to connect with others while still being myself.

Out of vulnerability, little by little, I have been incorporating a more optimistic discourse into my life: I now know that I'm worthy of good things, that I'm enough; that I'm, above all, vulnerable.

I guess quite a few people will ask themselves why write an autobiographical book, and what for, when I am only thirty-six years old—is it perhaps half of my life, maybe a third?—and with a seemingly successful life journey. I even ask myself this question. However, I feel some of my experience may, if not help, at least elicit curiosity. I believe in the autobiographical as the self-portrait of life in a precise moment, like climbing a mountain, stopping, breathing, and from there contemplating the landscape. I will come back to climb and look again, add fragments, to see from another perspective what I have lived. Maybe in thirty-six more years. Before. Later. I can't know.

"Vulnerability is the core, the heart, the center of meaningful human experiences," Brené Brown says. That's what I've believed in since before I knew I believed it. That's why I've kept journals since I was a child; that's why I've been writing non-stop for so long, giving words to my emotions.

As of now, this book is one of the forms of my vulnerability.

I run the risk—I assume it—of exposing the seams of who I have been and who I am, of revealing my dark side and my deepest fears, of leaving out in the open the reasons that have led me to sadness, traumas, and obsessions, to victimization, to painful love breakups, to drastic life changes.

I run the risk of revealing the processes that led me to suffer three severe depressions and even contemplate suicide.

I run the risk of drawing the attention of others to two conditions that few assume out loud—that

I'm a person with attention deficit disorder, and I'm a person with a hearing impairment.

I run the risk of being myself, more than the smiling beauty queen that turned up in newspapers, magazines, and videos, who, between triumphs and joys, lived through resounding failures; beyond the dentist I am today, the yoga, meditation, and mindfulness teacher I exhibit in my social networks as activities that mark my life project.

To stop fighting against my vulnerability is a way to strip myself of heavy clothes, masks, shames, armors. I want to believe it is a path to gratitude, to the enjoyment of the small and big opportunities life offers, to deep learning experiences, to personal growth, to maturity, to peace and happiness. I want to believe that I'm preparing myself to help others, to simply tell them it's worth it to take risks, to be vulnerable, to value, as Brené Brown says, "the beauty of cracks".

Here is my little story.

Here is the little story of my cracks and my vulnerability.

A PORTUGUESE HOME WITH CERTAINTY
IS CERTAINLY A PORTUGUESE HOME

1.

My story doesn't begin with my story.

As has happened to so many children and grandchildren and great-grandchildren of migrants who made their lives in Venezuela, I became a story after many journeys: my maternal grandparents' journey, my father's journey, my own journey. Journeys of water and land, but, most of all, of the soul.

All of us in my family have had dreams. To make them come true, we had to hold on to them. We traveled with emotions; although at first not entirely clear, they were always uplifting, ready for the best future, where memories would never be anchors, but teachings.

2.

My father left three times the port of Funchal, Madeira, all of them with deep sorrow, but with the certainty that there was a destiny to fulfill on the other side of the sea.

The first time he did it in 1963, at the age of thirteen. They had him board the Colonial Navigation Company's famous transatlantic liner Santa Maria, where most of the Portuguese headed to the Venezuelan port of La Guaira traveled, my maternal grandparents among them. On that ship, my father went all by himself, very sad, not knowing why he was being taken away from his family, why he had to go to another world. He couldn't understand then that, besides betting on the family fate of overcoming a precarious economic situation, he was fleeing from an age in which all Portuguese men were recruited for the army and sent to the so-called colonial or overseas wars, which took place in Africa between 1961 and 1974. Several of his friends and acquaintances had died in this way.

From the ship, my father wrote beautiful letters narrating his voyage and his loneliness.

He told—an image that has marked me very much—that when the ship set sail, he ran from third class to the deck. Toward the stern, he could see the island of Madeira as it got smaller and smaller until it disappeared. Toward the bow, he saw the open sea, with its greens and blues, generous, with a still invisible horizon called Venezuela, where two of his brothers were waiting for him. He arrived at the port of La Guaira on June 7, 1963. He wondered if one day he would return to his homeland.

The second time my father left the port of Funchal was ten years after his emigration to Venezuela. He had just experienced one of the saddest farewells of his life; my paternal grandfather, Antonio Ferreira, had been diagnosed with lung cancer. He was taken to Lisbon and was even treated with chemotherapy, but the doctors said there was nothing more to be done, and he wanted to return home on Christmas Eve, December 24, 1973.

That time, my dad went back to Madeira for a couple of months—his father was already in bed, very weak. He saw him for the last time before returning to Venezuela in January 1974. My grandfather passed away on November 22 of that same year, and my dad couldn't attend the funeral.

He returned to Madeira years later when his mother suffered a stroke. He was able to see her alive for a week.

It's usual in Portugal for parents to choose the order of their children's surnames. Traditionally, the mother's surname goes first, but the surname that is passed on to the following generations is the second one. That is why, though my grandfather is named Ferreira, my father and his brothers are named Gonçalves, like my grandmother.

4.

When I emigrated from Venezuela to the United States in 2012, I was alone.

By myself, like my dad when he crossed the ocean.

I knew, from my family, how hard it is to leave the land of one's birth. Many times I called home crying, saying I wanted to go back. My dad would reply:

"Take it easy, that's the migrant's life; everything will be fine."

I knew I had to be strong, just as my whole family had been strong enough to survive many different circumstances, past and present. It wasn't easy, but it was my reality, and it's what has allowed me, in a way, to learn to accept cultural differences, to believe in others, to adapt to very diverse situations.

5.

To reinvent myself, I have looked back. I keep doing it.

I didn't know my paternal grandparents, both from the island of Madeira. My grandfather, Antonio Ferreira, was born in Santa Maria Maior, in Funchal. My grandmother, Trinidad Gonçalves, was born in 1910 in Camacha, a municipality of Santa Cruz. When they married, they went to live in Santa Maria Maior, on a plot of land that my grandfather had bought with a brother and a cousin, where they grew a variety of vegetables and fruits and produced wine, not just for family consumption but also to sell at the Mercado dos Lavradores in downtown Funchal.

My Gonçalves-Ferreira grandparents suffered three losses before forming a family with ten children, seven men and three women, all born in Santa Maria Maior—Augusto, Maria Luisa, Humberto, Luís, José, Fernanda, Antonio (my dad), João, Fernando, and Bernadete. My dad was the eighth, along with his twin brother João, who has suffered hearing loss since he was five as a result of an allergic reaction to penicillin. Because of his deafness, he was also mute and never wanted to go to school, not even one offering special education. As an adult, my dad always went with him to help him complete elementary school. This disability meant my father always protected and helped him, with immense patience, to read and write. Leaving him behind in Portugal was another great pain.

Both my aunt Fernanda and my uncle José were born with retinitis pigmentosa, a rare, hereditary, degenerative disease that causes vision to be reduced until it's almost lost and the affected person can only see a pinpoint. The illnesses of my uncles José and João were an uphill struggle for the family, but at the same time, they saved them from going to war. My uncle Humberto went to the army, but because he was a telegrapher and could speak English, he was assigned to send messages in Morse code; that is why he stayed in an office in Lisbon, far from the battlefield.

My dad remembers that when he got out of school, he had to take care of the goats, pigs, and other animals that were raised for home consumption. He also worked delivering groceries from the market among the neighboring homes.

My dad was a very rebellious teenager; he would run away from school, climb mountains, swim in rivers, eat the fruits he found along the way, and steal others to take them to his siblings, keeping it a secret from his unknowing parents; it was the way they mitigated the hunger of those years.

At that time, they didn't even have enough money to buy shoes, and my dad walked long distances barefoot, almost always in very steep areas. He and all his siblings have had a very special intelligence that allowed them to be self-taught, excel, and achieve their goals. Although their parents had no formal education whatsoever, they always read a lot; they were naturally bright, assertive, and focused. I admire that my dad knows about everything, that he has so many interests.

6.

They say my grandfather Antonio Ferreira was
very kind; they say he helped everyone he could,
that he supported his own family and his extended
one, his brothers, his cousins. That's why he never
made a fortune, and that's also why he decided to
spend a long time in the island of Curaçao to work
and send money. That was during World War II.
The economic situation was very harsh all over
Europe.

Towards the end of the 50s, Antonio Ferreira
sold his market stall—Barraca 21—to be able to
travel to Venezuela and call his sons from there to
work with him.

In Caracas, my grandfather and my uncle
Humberto started a restaurant. Two years later, my
grandfather returned to Madeira to take care of the
family he had left there and was surprised by
cancer and then death.

My grandmother, Trinidad, on the other hand,
also worked the land, especially during the times

when my grandfather was far away. I can imagine her with all the longings of Portuguese women who spent years waiting for their sailor and fisherman husbands. Eternal waits, full of sadness, loneliness, and uncertainty, not knowing if their husbands would return home. That longing is in our DNA, part of our families, and our lives. It is a condition of melancholy we carry wherever we go.

7.

My maternal grandparents are also from Madeira.

They were both born in 1937 in Tabua, a municipality in Ribeira Brava, west of Funchal. My grandfather, João Gomez da Silva, was from a very influential family, while my grandmother, Laurinda Pestana Garcês Gomez, came from a humble family dedicated to agriculture.

My grandfather Gomez da Silva lost his father when he was only five years old, and it was his mother who took care of the family. There were seven siblings—six boys and one girl—and he was the middle brother. Like so many youngsters of that time, he was sent to Venezuela.

Before leaving Madeira, he had seen my grandmother; he found her beautiful, so he wrote to her saying he wanted to meet her. But the trip and other matters kept him from writing to her for a long time, so much so that my grandmother began to ask about him. Finally, at last, he wrote again and, as it happened in those times, they fell in love through letters that went back and forth between Venezuela and Portugal for two years.

When my grandfather finally returned to Madeira in 1959, it was to marry my grandmother.

My maternal grandparents traveled to Venezuela in 1960 on the same transatlantic liner that would later take my father, the Santa Maria; in those times, the journey took several weeks because it made a very long route that, after Vigo and Funchal, included stops in the ports of Tenerife, Miami, and Curaçao until finally reaching La Guaira.

As soon as they arrived in Caracas, my grandparents settled west of the city in an apartment belonging to my grandfather's older brother, who had emigrated to Venezuela years before. Sometime later, they were able to move to another apartment, also in the west, where my mother, Maria Ivonne Gomez Pestana, was born in 1963. She already had two older sisters, Irene and Mariette, and was followed by Silvia and Oswaldo, the younger children.

They were living in that apartment when the 1967 Caracas earthquake struck.

My mother remembers she was so small and scared that she hid under the ironing table, which was covered with a tablecloth, so her parents went around desperately without finding her. It was my grandmother's brother who found her and took her down the stairs.

My maternal grandfather started working with his brothers in a bar they had acquired in Bella Vista. In those times, there were no hours in my grandfather's day or weekends in his calendar for the family. He was a very hard-working man; he got home very late, and my grandmother, just like my paternal grandmother, felt that deep loneliness and longing, the Portuguese melancholy that we women from my family are.

When things got better, my grandfather and his brothers bought several properties, and in 1971 they opened Tostadas El Tropezón in Los Chaguaramos, one of the most traditional restaurants in Caracas, where professors and students from the Universidad Central de Venezuela used to go, a fixture of the town, the meeting place after baseball games at the university stadium. I can proudly say my grandparents, with their fondly remembered arepas, are part of the history of gastronomy and restaurants in the Venezuelan capital.

8.

In his early days in Caracas, my dad worked in a company that recycled bottles collected from restaurants. He also worked as an employee in a restaurant owned by his two brothers. Later they made him a partner in another restaurant they set up on Casanova Avenue, which they also sold to found Comercial Grandola in 1974, a company that supplied equipment for restaurants, bars, and the hotel and catering industry.

At that point, Fernando, my father's younger brother, had also arrived in Venezuela. Once they were four, things got complicated, and my dad decided to stand aside; he entered into a partnership with an Italian man in a restaurant in the Campo Alegre neighborhood, which still exists.

My dad and my mom met in 1984. She was twenty years old, and my dad was thirty-four, a considerable difference at that time. She was studying Administration and Computer Science at Caracas University College.

My dad had seen her at a party and was captivated by her beauty. There he approached her and called her "skinny"; she turned around, and he took a rose, kissed it, and tossed it to her in the air.

They started talking and dating behind my grandfather's back. My grandfather didn't want his daughters to have boyfriends, so my dad would look for my mom at the university, they would have coffee, and he would drop her off near her house, never at the door, so my grandfather wouldn't find out. One day my dad told my mom:

"I'm too old for this show; what do I have to do for your dad to accept me?"

"Marry me," was my mom's answer.

My dad had no objection.

He was about to leave for four days with some friends for the Carnival in Rio de Janeiro and said that as soon as he returned, he would talk to my grandfather. Two weeks went by without my mom hearing anything from him: she says she was furious, thinking she had lost him. But as soon as he returned from Brazil, he called her and showed up at her house to ask for her hand. Against all odds, my grandfather had no qualms, and my grandmother only warned:

"Whoever comes to my house for one of my daughters has no turning back."

After six months of dating, my parents got married in 1984.

I was born in 1986, and my brother Tony in 1987.

My dad didn't want my mom to stay in college, and she reluctantly gave in. To this day, that is a constant issue at home, especially with me: that's why my mom insists that I be a professional, that I don't set aside my plans for anyone, least of all for a partner; that I be independent.

9.

We've been a close-knit family.

In Caracas, we had a fully Portuguese life. My grandparents spoke to me in Portuguese; we ate dishes from their land. On Sundays, we always had lunch together at my grandmother's house. And together, we lived the melancholy, the yearning for Portuguese traditions, for that other, far away homeland where we only went on vacation. It's curious that, being so happy to be in Madeira, my parents did not want to stay there. I felt immensely free in Funchal; we ran through the fields and forests, we entered the neighbors' homes, the streets seemed clean and tidy to me. We didn't feel the fear and insecurity that tormented us so much in Caracas; as a child, I used to tell my parents that everything was perfect there, that we should stay there forever.

On the other hand, we didn't spend vacations in Venezuela—we didn't know other cities. While my school friends went to the mountains of Merida or the beaches of Margarita Island, we never traveled around the country. My dad was afraid of the roads and the insecurity. I only got to see the inner country when I was Miss Venezuela. That was contradictory, because at school we learned and practiced Venezuelan traditions, we ate many local dishes that were the specialty of my family's restaurants. And despite that, at school, they bullied me by calling me "la portu", emphasizing stigmas that have always been ascribed to the Portuguese in Venezuela about their smell or their trades.

All this generated in me a deep estrangement, a sort of duality.

I felt equally Venezuelan and Portuguese, but amid great confusion. It was a bit like being in prison without the possibility of choosing a more neutral, free space. Now my own migration has added to this, and it has been very painful for me to have to just say I'm Portuguese in order not to experience the rejection that often occurs when I say I'm Venezuelan, something that is happening to Venezuelans in many corners of the world.

It has been very tough, it seems unfair and even shameful to deny my Venezuelan nationality to get a job, but I've had to do it.

Only today, I'm a little more at peace with these issues of identity.

I can say, without resentment, that I am fifty percent Venezuelan and fifty percent Portuguese. In balance. This is reflected in my daily life. On a Sunday, I can prepare arepas while listening to fados. I can be happy and serene, and yet melancholic, with that Portuguese longing of my grandmothers and their mothers and grandmothers.

BAREFOOT I COME,
FROM THE FAR REACHES OF CHILDHOOD

1.

I was a child locked in a tower.

I remember looking out from the apartment where we lived in the Santa Paula neighborhood in southeast Caracas. I would see the neighborhood children playing in the park. I'd open the window of my room, and from there, on the tenth floor, I'd shout, tell them things, pretend to play with them.

Once, I caught their attention and announced I'd give them a flute concert. I played several pieces for them. On another occasion, I showed them my parrot, which flew half-heartedly in the afternoon breeze. Perhaps they never saw me, let alone heard me.

I never understood why my parents strictly forbade me to spend time with the building's other children and also with those at school. I would complain, and they would tell me:

"Be grateful to God; at your age, they wouldn't even let me go out to the playground."

My parents were very overprotective, so much so that they never let me or my brother go out alone. Never to a schoolmate's home, never to a party, much less to a sleepover at a friend's. Furthermore, there was the belief that women were exposed to many things and had to be locked up and protected. It was subjugation and machismo, no doubt. Today I see my father's overprotective character had to do with his own history, with the troubles at his home in Madeira, the absence of his parents, the forced migration as a child, the fact that he was raised by his brothers.

There was also, for a long time, a sort of negative reinforcement from my mother due to her own history of how her mother and sisters were raised, which was also in a Portuguese, macho, overprotected way. My mom gave body and soul to my brother and me: she cooked by herself; she lived to take care of us. She did it the way she could, the way she knew.

Both my mother and my father were repeating behaviors they weren't aware of; they were only making sure nothing awful would happen to me. This has all reflected in me in many different ways, perhaps in the fact that I run away when someone tries to control me; that I can't stand being bossed around; that in personal relationships, I often felt I was required to sacrifice something of myself in order to obtain affection and retribution.

All this has made me an introverted, insecure, dependent person.

It's a pattern I'm working on, and a difficult one at that, but it makes me who I am.

2.

I spent all my elementary and high school at Colegio San Luis, in the San Luis neighborhood, in El Cafetal. It was a big middle-class institution for boys and girls, with classrooms for fifty to sixty students. I didn't go to a more select school or an all-girls school because this one was very close to my home and allowed my brother and I to study together.

My brother, barely a year younger than me, paid the consequences of my refusal to be confined. I always wanted to play, to move, to share. He, on the other hand, spent hours immobile, devoted to videogame consoles. I would come in, stand in front of the TV and dance. Then I would look for a hat and continue dancing. First, he'd say to me, "Move over." Then, "Move, or I'll beat you up." And I'd go back in, and, of course, he'd get furious. I'd come back and turn off the Nintendo and run away. All that, just to get his

31

attention and get him to play with me. We fought a lot, like all siblings.

We slept in the same room until I was about seven years old. All his toy cars were there, lots of pictures, the trophies and medals we had won in sports. And my dolls were also there, but my mom never let me play with those Barbies; they were forbidden ornaments. I had a lot of them; there were some with spectacular dresses, and I never got to play with them. It never occurred to me to defy my mother, to break a doll, play hide and seek. I was very obedient, I had a lot of respect for my parents, and also a lot of fear.

When we moved to Los Naranjos, I had my own room. There, I fulfilled my dream of having a desk of my own. Until then, we had always done our homework in the kitchen. I wanted that desk to write at.

I spent hours and hours writing diaries in which I wrote about everything that happened to me, from the simplest things, like buying a cookie, to the most important events. I also wrote about my emotions. The things I kept to myself, my repressed feelings, I wrote them all down. In addition, I decorated those journals with drawings, glitter. I was very skilled in crafts.

My diaries had special corners to write the most precious secrets; they remained sealed with a sticker. I would seal them with crazy glue so that my secrets would be even more protected, even from myself.

One day, when I was about fifteen years old, I found my mother sitting on my bed reading my diaries. I cried, I complained, we argued. There it was, written in great detail, how much I liked—since I can remember, I'd say —a boy from the Portuguese Center, the one who would be my first boyfriend.

The Portuguese mentality made us think that this first boyfriend had to be the one we would marry and be happy with forever. That was what happened to many of my friends. Not to me.

3.

I was about eleven years old when my dad started bringing my brother and me along to work in his restaurant during all the vacations we stayed in Caracas.

My first job was washing glasses; then I made juice, picked up plates, did duties as a waitress. My dad used to tell us we had to know how to do everything, that in a restaurant, you start with the basics, as he himself started.

It was around the age of fifteen when he finally allowed me to work the cash register. But that didn't last long. One day a man wanted to give me a box of chocolates, and my dad thought it was wrong. He never let me go again.

4.

The only place of freedom I experienced as a child and teenager was the Portuguese Center. It was like being outside Venezuela and, at the same time, at home, a protective space apart from reality. That's why my parents enrolled me in every possible activity. I would leave school, have lunch at home, do my homework, and my mom would take us there. I would spend the whole afternoon there, and also on weekends.

I did swimming, karate, tennis. I was very good at tennis; I got to be federated, and if I had put myself to it, I would have been a tennis player, perhaps of international stature. But when tennis started to be a serious activity and required me to leave the walls of the Portuguese Center to attend interclub tournaments or travel outside Caracas, my parents were against it. That was the end of their support. Again, overprotection made its appearance, and with it, the ghosts of dangerous roads, of what could happen to me in contact with other people.

I was good at sports because I was very competitive. I still am. Competitive with myself, never with others. I set myself goals and was obsessed with achieving them. That's why sports never helped me socialize, which would seem the obvious thing. That's why, despite sports, I was very lonely as a child; I had few friends.

5.

For my dad, nothing was enough.

Not even my good grades in school, not even my success in sports.

I'd come home excited with my report card, and my dad would just say:

"It's just your duty."

When I got home with my tennis trophies and medals, he would only comment:

"That's what you practice so much for; it's normal for you to do well."

Never any congratulations. Never words of pride or encouragement.

I saw how my cousins and friends were celebrated for their small triumphs, and I wasn't. It hurt me; it made everything a sacrifice for me, a tremendous effort; it made me feel I was never good enough as a daughter, as a sister, as a friend.

I still feel I have to make an extra effort to please.

I forgave my dad a long time ago. I accepted his reasons and reconciled myself with his way of being, the only way he has to express his love for us.

Around the age of 22, I ended up rebelling, taking charge of my life.

One night, I went to a party. The phone was bursting with calls from my parents that I didn't answer. I came home at about four in the morning and found my dad awake; he scolded me and asked me:

"Do you think this is nice? Do you think what you're doing makes sense?"

"Well, yes," I answered.

There were long, tragic faces all weekend as if the world had ended. I ended up telling my parents I was tired of feeling subdued, suffocated. I told them they should trust me more because I always told them everything about my life, absolutely everything; we even talked about topics that were lurid or taboo for other families. I think fluid communication with parents is very important. It was my dad who fostered that openness in my home, and that's what allows me to talk to them and other people straight from the heart, with vulnerability on edge.

6.

At school, I also had very few friends.

I was studying with so many people, yet I only met with a small group of five or six classmates, always the same ones, from the time we started elementary school until we graduated from high school. Some of us even went to college together.

While everyone played and ran around the playground, we stayed on the stairs. I, in particular, had a hard time interacting with others; I was very shy, awkward, introverted. Even in college, I blushed when I asked for water; my voice would not come out.

I never liked to draw attention to myself, to be the center of anything.

I remember when I was in fourth grade, my mother said she was going to switch us to a better school, my brother to a boys' school, and me to an all-girls school. I cried, I cried a lot; I begged them not to do it because my friends were all in San Luis, and I was happy there. They finally didn't switch us.

7.

I have what they call attention deficit hyperactivity disorder: ADHD. I suspected it, but I was diagnosed very recently, when I was already living in the United States.

When I started studying English in Miami, I wondered why it was so hard for me, why I had to concentrate so much. I discussed it with a professor, who quickly said that my problem was not with English and recommended that I see a psychologist at the language institute.

I was evaluated, and it was determined that I'm a person with mild ADHD.

After the diagnosis, I began to study what ADHD is all about, how to live with it, and I took on the task of reviewing my entire life as a student, which made me understand many things. I remember it took me hours to memorize subjects that took others a moment. My good grades came exclusively from my willpower, from the fact that I invested hours and hours in memorizing with a superhuman effort. In college, it was no different, but I already had the training from school, and it never seemed to me that this wasn't normal. My parents and teachers didn't notice any unusual behavior either because I wasn't hyperactive, which in the past was a symptom associated with this condition.

ADHD now explains my manual agility, my love of jewelry, details, and also sports.

I think of Michael Phelps, the great Olympic medalist. He was diagnosed with attention deficit hyperactivity disorder (ADHD) in sixth grade and found that he could not sit still in the classroom but instead could swim for three hours straight. In his book *Beneath the Surface*, he reveals that when he discovered swimming, he felt free: "I could swim fast in the pool, partly because being there calmed my mind. In the water, I felt in control for the first time."

8.

Ever since I was a child, I had a particular weakness for underprivileged children, the bullied ones, for instance. I befriended them, defended them, formed study groups with them; I tried to help them integrate, to make others accept them.

In 2020, at the beginning of the covid-19 pandemic lockdown, I started posting on my Instagram account some recommendations on how to get active at home. Some former classmates from school began to show up, including a guy who told me out of the blue he wanted to thank me. I had no idea why. It was for having defended him at school, for having been his friend when everyone tried to abuse him for being overweight. I couldn't believe he remembered me so many years later for that. A former classmate had also shown up on Facebook; many kids rejected her because she dressed like a boy. I befriended her anyway, cared for her, defended her. Today he is a transgender man, and he thanked me for those times of

43

solidarity and support. It was touching because I did it without expecting anything in return.

If I have to search for where my empathy with people comes from—it remains intact to this day—I must say it stems from my family. From my grandfather, who helped many people in Madeira. From my dad, who was always very special with his employees, helping and supporting them. I grew up seeing that; I grew up knowing that being helpful begets happiness in others and oneself. It was one of the reasons why I decided to study dentistry, a career that would allow me to heal others and be helpful.

MY LIFE IS REBORN

IN THIS WOUNDED CORNER OF MINE

1.

As a child, when someone asked me what I'd study when I grew up, I always said I wished to heal people, so we all assumed I'd choose medicine.

When, at the end of high school, I had to make a decision, I stopped to think that medicine was a beautiful profession but a very demanding one—six years of studies, then rural medicine, then the specialty. Even then, I was sure I wanted to get married and have children. It was a goal. I couldn't imagine all that was about to happen to me that would lead me to think that perhaps the time for all that had already passed and I'd be the first to be surprised if one day it happened. Anyway, my choice was between Pharmacy and Dentistry.

I ended up deciding on dentistry because it had to do with taking care of people. That was exactly what I cared about. Besides, I thought it was a career that would allow me to be my own boss, manage my time so as not to stop playing sports, run my home, and take care of my children.

I studied at Santa Maria University in Caracas. I would have liked to study at the Central University of Venezuela, but there was a limit on Dentistry admission quotas at that time, and it was almost obligatory to apply for Biology or Chemistry and then ask for a switch. It was a waste of time. Besides, that university was gigantic; its spaces were overwhelming to me.

For me, coming from so much confinement, college was a threat.

Six former classmates from San Luis School studied dentistry with me from the first day of the course until we graduated. They were among my best and closest friends, the ones I had been with since preschool. That made me feel more comfortable and accompanied. Some of them are still close friends today.

Santa Maria is a private university; dentistry materials are expensive. At that time, my father had made the decision to remodel the restaurant and buy the apartment we had moved to. The first two years of my career were difficult and involved many sacrifices for the family and hard work in the restaurant. My dad was supportive; all he said to me was, "I hope you won't disappoint me."

I loved the career since day one. I felt I was studying something right for me, something I was passionate about. I have always been interested in science, and I believe almost all the answers we are looking for are there, including those that connect us with spirituality.

Since the first year of college, we had to see patients, so I had family members, friends, and employees of my father's restaurant as patients, and Rosy, who has been cleaning my house since I was seven years old. Rosy helped me get many patients; she took her family and acquaintances from Petare, the neighborhood where she lived, one of the largest in Latin America. It made more sense to me to help those who could hardly afford to pay for dental treatments like the ones I could give them for free.

Those patients often arrived at my office tired, sweaty, late, due to Caracas' transportation problems. Then one day, I began to pick them up myself with an old car my mother lent me, an '86 Toyota Corolla Avila. I'd go into the neighborhood, pick them up and often take them back. When we left late, I'd ask them if they had eaten. We'd stop at a McDonald's, and we'd all eat. That little gesture filled me with happiness. My parents didn't find out about it until long after I graduated, when they could no longer worry or scold me.

I still get e-mails today from people who were my patients, asking me if I'll return to Venezuela, if I'll be able to treat them again someday. They tell me their crowns, fixed dentures, resins, and other treatments I performed on them are still in perfect condition. I guess I always sought to generate connections with my patients, bonds from life itself. Before I started attending them in the clinic, I listened to their problems, they told me about their lives.

I strove a lot to practice dentistry. A lot.

2.

Not everything was a bed of roses while I studied at the university.

In the meantime, I lived through one of the darkest times of my life.

I was still dating the Portuguese boy I had liked since childhood; I had begun a relationship with him when I was sixteen.

Towards the end of my first year in college, on Holy Week, I traveled with my parents to Bariloche, Argentina. My boyfriend would travel to the beaches of Tucacas with some friends. At that time, the only form of digital communication at hand was Messenger, and it always had to be used from a computer. In the hotel, as you would expect, there were computers for guests, so I started exchanging messages with him. But one day I wrote to him and he didn't answer. I called him on the phone and he didn't answer either. I started to despair; I panicked. There was no way to talk to him.

One night, even though I knew it was wrong, I tried several passwords and managed to get into his Messenger account and see all the conversations he was having. One of them was with a girl who was showing him pictures in swimsuits and asking him which one to take to the beach where they were going together. He was being unfaithful to me.

We had been dating for six years.

It drove me crazy.

I was in a wonderful place, with spectacular mountains and lakes, and my mind and heart were spinning about what was killing me and what I knew was the end of the relationship.

I took captures of all the conversations that proved the infidelity, printed them out, and put them in a folder that traveled with me back to Caracas.

The Monday after that Holy Week, I confronted him. I first gave him the gift I had bought him in Argentina—I remember it was a wooden carving with the figure of a surfer—and I confronted him:

"Don't you have anything to tell me?"

He said no, and said I looked weird.

Finally, I handed him the folder and asked him to examine it, to take his time and process everything in it. As he shouted that I was crazy, I asked him to get out of my car and was emphatic:

"You've lost me forever; don't come looking for me again; you're dead to me, completely dead."

3.

My heart was shattered.

I came home crying and kept on crying for many days.

For me, it was more than the breakup with a first boyfriend. More than the deception, it was about everything he meant to me, the world we had built, outside of which nothing else existed. It was understood that we would get married, that we would form a home. I lost my virginity to him. I had never imagined my life without him and even less with another person. Within the ways of our Portuguese families, there was no other possibility but to stay together. And now it was all over, and I was not about to forgive him.

Three weeks later, he started looking for me. He asked for my forgiveness, said I was the woman of his life, he had made a mistake, he missed me. He would show up at the university, at my house, everywhere. He had engaged in a form of stalking that had me very overwhelmed.

One day he came to the university with a small box and a ring. He asked me to marry him. I told him no, he had done something unforgivable that would not be solved with that ring.

The last thing I said to him was:

"I want nothing more to do with you. Don't ever look for me again; you're dead to me."

4.

A week later, at midnight, my phone rang.

It was a friend of his. There was a lot of noise, but I could hear:

"Vanessa, he's dead. Please help me."

I didn't know what I had heard, I didn't want to understand, I couldn't. The friend was calling me in front of the corpse of the man who had been my boyfriend until a few days before. He was still in the Altamira area, in Caracas, where he had been in a traffic accident.

I took a deep breath. I woke up my brother, who was a close friend of his.

I took a deep breath. We woke up my parents. My dad and brother got dressed and went to the site of the accident.

I took a deep breath. I called his sister; she asked me to call her dad. It was a terrible moment. When I heard his voice on the other end of the phone, I barely hinted that his son had been in a very serious accident. I didn't have the strength to tell him the truth.

5.

On the day of the funeral, his mother hugged me and said:

"Forgive him."

It was all very confusing. She felt a lot of guilt for what her son had done to me, and I also felt guilty for having told her several times that he was dead to me.

Now he was dead for real.

That's how I stumbled into what I'd heard people call "depression". My first depression.

6.

I suspected many of the women who stopped by the funeral parlor of having had something with my ex-boyfriend. In fact, I was sure of it.

The months and years that followed were very tough.

I went through my second and third years of college with great sadness and depression. I would go to the cemetery every Friday to bring him a daisy. He loved daisies. It was my way of unburdening myself, of understanding, of living my grief.

A Friday, as I was walking to the grave, I saw a young woman standing there.

I recognized her immediately: she was the one in Messenger, the one with the bathing suit and the infidelity.

I turned around and started walking very fast towards the car. She called out to me:

"Vanessa, Vanessa. Please forgive me."

I kept walking, and before I left, I only managed to say, "Can you come another day, not Friday?"

7.

At the Portuguese Center, I went from being a future wife to being a widow.

I became invisible. Never again did a man of Portuguese descent dare to look at me. No one asked me out, not even for an ice cream. That was very hard because I didn't move in other social circles.

I became more and more lonely.

Looking back, I can assume that he and I would have talked and reconciled. Most likely, I would have forgiven him and continued with the tradition. Maybe I would still be married to him, having children, enduring who knows how many infidelities in a relationship that, sexually, was always very unhappy, even though he was a kind and loving guy.

At that moment, I did forgiveness therapy. I forgave him and forgave myself. I took everything that happened as a very powerful life lesson, a piece of knowledge that today makes me sure that in a relationship, there must be passion, love, respect, and peace in equal measures.

8.

Because of my grief, I stopped enjoying many things in my dental career.

It was a severe blow. Everything became very hard for me. I spent a lot of time going from home to the university and back. Isolated. Locked up. The freedom I had gained from my parents, I took it away from myself.

I became very thin; I stopped doing physical training.

I was twice in mourning: from the relationship and from the death. And I was not aware at the time of the importance of living through all the stages of grief.

Toward the end of my studies, I had to do internships and a rotating residency; I enjoyed it a little more, mainly because it had to do with my fondness for volunteering. I treated patients in different social institutions and public hospitals in many different areas of Caracas, especially in poor neighborhoods with very precarious conditions, where dental health was the least important thing and people were already in a lot of pain. We helped HIV patients and people with disabilities, children, the elderly.

I spent the three months of the rotating residency, or rural practice, in Higuerote, a coastal town in the Barlovento area, well known for its beaches and drumming bands. I was there with my friend Verusska, my classmate since kindergarten. For me, who had never left Caracas, that was a vital experience. The Higuerote General Hospital was then an incredible place, with doctors of immense vocation. The townsfolk were very kind, warm, and grateful.

The final stretch of college was a very demanding experience, particularly the elective subject of Forensic Dentistry, which we attended at the National Headquarters of Medicine and Forensic Science, known simply as the Bello Monte Morgue. It wasn't a mandatory subject, but if I took it, it would pave the way to the postgraduate course I wanted to pursue in Bogota.

That morgue stirred my emotions; I knew my boyfriend had been there after the accident; his body had been moved through those same corridors where I was walking, leading to the autopsy room.

I saw terrible things in that place, people crying and screaming, waiting for news of their dead; also, lonely corpses that no one claimed or that couldn't be identified—because they were burned or deformed—which I had to handle to take a dental impression.

Corpses arrived which had been stabbed, shot, torn apart by the violence of the city. The smell of the dead is a smell of emptiness; I couldn't explain it any other way. And that's what was there. The dead were numbers, meat thrown on the floor, or on metal stretchers, with no regard for human dignity. The quality of the autopsies depended on whether a family was paying or not. Chests were sewn with wick because there was no money for surgical thread.

9.

Finally, in 2009, after a lot of physical and emotional effort, I received my dental degree.

For me, it was a goal accomplished, a momentous achievement. I was very excited because, at some point, I had thought I wouldn't make it.

I already had plans for my future in the field. I was thrilled.

So, what did my dad tell me at that moment? The usual: "It's just your duty."

BEAUTY IS THE NAME

OF SOMETHING THAT DOESN'T EXIST

1.

As soon as I graduated from college, I prepared to travel to Bogota and take a three-month diploma course in Aesthetic Dentistry and Smile Design with the Colombian Society of Aesthetic Dentistry and the Graduate School of the San Martin University Foundation. It would allow me to enter directly into a master's degree at the Universidad Javeriana.

It was my aspiration.

I was still interested in everything that had to do with meticulous handicrafts. That's why I had my own line of jewelry with the VAGG seal, which I started making to sell at school, at the Portuguese Center, then at the university, in bazaars, and later taking commissions for corporate gifts. I did very well with that. Hence, smile design and aesthetic dentistry suited precisely what I liked. I can proudly say my dental crowns were perfect.

When I returned from Colombia, I started working.

I had a small office in a building in Los Ruices. There I saw patients from early morning until almost dusk.

As I had done all my life, I played sports and trained.

I'd get up at five in the morning, go to the gym before six in the morning, and by seven-thirty, I was showered and wearing my uniform, ready to go to the office.

One morning, as I was leaving the gym in the Macaracuay shopping center, one of the trainers came up to me and asked me out of the blue:

"Would you like to be in the Miss Venezuela pageant?"

I looked at him, somewhat in horror, and quickly answered no, that world had nothing to do with me. He wanted me to have a conversation with him; I rushed away, telling him I was running late.

The next day, he approached me again with the same question. It was Richard Linares, a well-known coach, motivator, expert in training pageant candidates. He was the official coach for the Miss Venezuela pageant. Once again, I answered that I wasn't interested at all and, besides, I was too old for a beauty contest; I was twenty-four years old, and those contests are usually entered by seventeen- and eighteen-year-old girls.

But he insisted; he said he saw a lot of potential in me. Every time we met, it was the same old song and dance.

One day I couldn't train in the morning because I had an early appointment with a patient, and since I was a little afraid to go to the gym at night, I asked my mom to go with me. As soon as we walked in, we ran into Linares, who was full of compliments for my mom, who looks quite spectacular and very well preserved—there was a time when they asked us if we were sisters.

As you would expect, Richard told my mom about his intentions to take me to Miss Venezuela. As soon as we got home that night, my mom told my dad, called my aunts, my grandmother. Everyone was excited, and I didn't understand why. That pageant meant absolutely nothing to me; it had never crossed my mind to compete and even less to win. Physical training and good nutrition were part of my life routine, with no interests beyond health and feeling good. Exercise and sports, since I was a child, were a form of catharsis to fill me with energy and sometimes a form of escape.

A few days later, I went back to the gym with my mom and aunt. And, of course, there was Richard Linares. Now I had two very interested parties convinced that I should not miss such an opportunity. I fled to the cardiovascular area, one floor up. When I returned, they were with one of Osmel Sousa's assistants, whom they had made go just to see me.

2.

A week later, I stood, still not very convinced, at the Miss Venezuela Headquarters. They ushered me into Osmel Sousa's office, a space full of crowns, ribbons, handkerchiefs, flowered fabrics; everything I was not. Next to him were his assistants, Harry Levy and Carlos Luis Angel, and Maria Kallay, the pageant's coordinator.

It was a very weird moment.

I kept wondering what I was doing there, why I answered so meekly to every question about my life, my history, why I wore a bathing suit to be examined. I had agreed to go merely to understand what it was all about and mostly, I admit, to calm the family frenzy. I was also hugely curious to meet the so-called Beauty Czar.

I explained I had never modeled before and didn't know how to pose or walk down a catwalk.

"Don't worry, this is Beauty University; if you win, a thousand doors will open for you," they answered.

I also made it clear to them that I had a job, that I had responsibilities in my practice. They convinced me by assuring me it would take a couple of hours once a week and only for three months, the months remaining for the 2010 competition.

Finally, I agreed to participate with the condition that if I didn't feel well or didn't like the process, I would withdraw. I made it a point not to take patients on Thursdays and to train even more intensely in the gym, as they asked me to do.

I chose to be Miss Miranda because it's the state where I was born.

At home, inexplicably, they went crazy with the news. They were happy and excited as I never saw them, not even when I graduated as a dentist.

3.

I remember the first meeting with the twenty-eight girls who participated in the contest, each one more beautiful than the other, each one thinner than the other, all spectacular. There were a lot of people who were part of the pageant team.

Someone suddenly asked me who had taken me there. I naively answered:

"Myself, with my car."

"No, honey, who's your representative, your modeling agency."

They couldn't believe I was there only because Richard Linares had seen me in a gym. I remember they made me walk, stop at three points and go on.

As I was leaving, Gisselle Reyes, the modeling teacher, complained to me:

"Boy, am I going to have a hard time with you!"

Thus began some very hard weeks that I set myself to face with dedication, with sacrifice, again bearing over my shoulders the complexes that made me tell myself that I wasn't good for that, that

I had to push myself to the limit. I only took comfort in the assumption that everything I was doing would have some benefit, that I would learn something from the many hours I spent in classes on general culture, public speaking, verbalization, diction, speech therapy, dance, English, catwalk, theater, photo posing, styling, make-up.

Almost the first thing they asked me to do was to stop weight training because my body looked like a bodybuilder's and not like a pageant queen's. They controlled my food, my weight, my measurements. Close to the presentation to the press, they suggested me a little touch-up on my nasal septum, which in any case, I should have had operated before because I had it a little deviated, and it generated sinusitis. That was all. I had perfect teeth, and I had already enlarged my breasts when I was twenty years old—the disproportion between my hips and a completely flat chest bothered me. I had a minor breast surgery without my parents' consent and paid for the surgery with my own savings because I always worked and always had savings—I remember that, in addition to jewelry, I sold CDs at school with selections of fashionable music that I burned myself.

What started out as a single day dedicated to the contest turned into two, three, five, then the whole week without a break.

I was forced to leave my practice.

Even then, without knowing anything about mindfulness, I had already perceived what a British monk said to Shauna Shapiro in Thailand, which she often repeats: "If you practice it, you reinforce it." When I take on a responsibility, I force myself to do everything perfectly, to completely fulfill it, to never fail. I practice and practice to reinforce what I can and can't do, what comes naturally to me, and what is difficult.

I didn't miss any rehearsal; I took care of myself; I kept training.

I took it as I take almost everything in life: as a job.

4.

At that time, I was 1.76 centimeters tall (5'9")
and weighed 54 kilos (119,05 lb); I was very thin. It
was part of my genetics but also a consequence of
uncontrolled diets in which I ate only fish and no
carbohydrates. Sometime later, that had a rebound
effect and repercussions on my health.

My measurements for Miss Venezuela were
92-60-92; then, for Miss Universe, they changed a
little because the required stereotype was different,
less fitness, more natural.

At the so-called Beauty Gala, a TV program
that aired twelve days before the Miss Venezuela
show, the first special awards were presented, and
I won the Best Body Sash. I took it as a prize for the
many years I had been exercising and doing sports.
It was also a confirmation that taking care of my
body was a path that I shouldn't abandon.

The transformation into Miss Venezuela
implied I had to dye my hair blonde. I had kept it
virgin until then. And I had to sunbathe every day;

they wanted to turn me into a tan blonde. The pageant turns women into a performance; they create a new personality for you. I, the introvert, endured the sacrifice of giving up being myself; I gave in and let them build me into an extroverted, light, carefree, slightly mannered character.

I was a fiction.

I kept asking myself what it was all for, to please whom. Of course, I was sacrificing myself to please my family, in order to compete with myself, as I had done in sports. In order not to fail, not to fail me.

5.

At Miss Venezuela, I made incredible friends. I'm still in contact with some of them; as a group, we had no major conflicts or scandals. I was amazed by the stories from some girls from the inner country, from very humble and even violent homes, who were in the contest almost as their only option for social mobility, hoping for a change of life, and with many difficulties to get the clothes, shoes, and jewelry they had to wear. It was a reality completely unknown to me until then and made me appreciate my heritage, the values I was given at home. Added to that was another complex environment—television, modeling, egos.

We had to be polished in many aspects and undergo a great deal of strictness to make the grade. Maria Kallay called me every day to make sure I had gone to the gym, to class. I, who had managed to free myself from my parents' grip, was controlled again at all hours and by strangers.

One day I dared to tell Maria Kallay to leave me alone, that I was no longer a child, that I was in the contest with a real sense of responsibility. Later we became very dear friends, and I owe her a lot; I felt sorry for her passing.

Modeling was the one aspect that was really uphill for me. I took private lessons with Gisselle Reyes, who was concerned about my age and my absolute lack of catwalk know-how. She didn't like me very much at first, but later, she was also very friendly and approachable.

Many things are said about Miss Venezuela. I didn't see them or live them. I only saw hard-working people determined to make things go well. I never perceived rivalries among the contestants, straddling, favoritism. There's also a lot of talk about Osmel Sousa, but I only saw a strict person who made the contest his life and bet everything on it.

6.

Before Miss Venezuela, I never thought of beauty as a physical concept. I knew I was pretty, yes, but not more than other women. I didn't consider it an advantage. I didn't care about it. I didn't use it. Instead, my insecurity made me assume I wasn't physically special. I went through times when I felt too skinny or too tall or self-conscious because I had no breasts. I lived in dissatisfaction, disliking myself, in permanent anxiety.

The maturity I had at the time of Miss Venezuela was what allowed me to become aware that it was precisely that maturity that constituted my weapon, that the security that age gave me was beauty in itself. It's reflected in the way I walk, in my presence, in everything.

Taking care of your body isn't worshipping it.

Looking good is a form of integrity.

Unlike in those times, today I don't go on diets; I enjoy eating very much. I just set limits; I avoid excesses. I love sweets almost obsessively. Sometimes it's not easy for me to control that addiction; sometimes, I can eat a jar of ice cream. But I try to balance health and pleasure. Pleasure is fundamental. There will always be a next day to make up for the excesses.

I prepare myself for old age, for the day when the beauty and elasticity of the body come to an end. Exercising, more than beauty, means taking care of the musculature that supports the skeletal system. I also prepare myself by knowing how human beings function hormonally and neurologically.

I want to reach old age in good health. Health is beauty.

Today I feel like never before, comfortable in my body and in my skin.

7.

In 2010, the fifty-seventh edition of the Miss
Venezuela pageant was held on Thursday, October
28, at the Palacio de Eventos, which was part of the
Crowne Plaza Maruma Hotel in Maracaibo. It was
the first time it was held outside Caracas, which
implied a whole logistics operation, not just for me
as a contestant but also for my family. I was
accompanied by my parents, my brother, my aunts,
my godparents, my cousins, and my boyfriend at
the time, a Portuguese boy who had dared to break
the dreadful curse that had made me the widow of
my first boyfriend.

In Maracaibo, everything happened very fast,
like in a movie.

The Gran Salón Venezuela was packed. It was
a very diversified program, with a lot of talent from
the region; the presenters donned beautiful and
shiny guajira robes. The most relevant gaita singers
of the moment were there—Neguito Borjas, Betulio
Medina, Ricardo Cepeda, and Gustavo Aguado—

and even Lila Morillo and her daughters Liliana and Lilibeth took part. It was a Zulian party in tribute to the gaita and the Wayúu people. Mixed within a spectacular choreography, the participants also sang and danced. My character danced and sang.

The stage was completely different from the one where we had rehearsed back in Caracas; there were thousands of stairs, and I just prayed to God not to let me fall, not to let my high heels get tangled.

In the middle of the event, I decided I wouldn't make my entrance where we had been pointed out during the rehearsals, because of the thousand stairs and the blinding lights. I went out the other way, so I wouldn't fall and make a fool of myself. In fact, that night, many girls stumbled and slipped. It was really hard.

A certain amount of bullying on the contestants of a beauty pageant is usually assumed as natural, especially at the time of the round of questions. The criticisms are acid and inclement. Few stop to think that at that time, fatigue and stress are at their peak, as is the pressure, for it is "the hour of truth"; many girls don't eat anything that day for fear of gaining a few grams. In addition, there's the lights, the people shouting, the fear of making a mistake, of looking foolish.

I was asked which profession a woman should never work in. I remember exactly what I answered: "I believe a woman doesn't have to set limits on her profession because, in this day and age, women are capable of achieving realization in any type of profession; that's why we're fighters and entrepreneurs, and we can be mothers and professionals at the same time." I still think that way. We're capable of everything at the same time—and well.

In order to comply with that moment of questions, the participants had previously been given a lot of topics to study. I practiced a lot; I made my parents ask me questions over and over again. I prepared myself a lot, especially to face my shyness and be able to make my words come out in front of the thousands of people who would be watching the event that night at the venue and on television. José Rafael Briceño, the so-called Professor Briceño, prepared us for the questions, gave us tips on how to put together an answer and a coherent speech. I owe it to Miss Venezuela to have helped me to confront my fears, to develop strategies to express myself, and to appear more confident.

8.

I had psyched myself up to be the first finalist.

I wanted to go to Miss World, a quieter pageant, without major consequences. I wanted to end that quickly and resume my plans for graduate school in Bogota. In fact, shortly before Miss Venezuela, I had completed an online interview with the Universidad Javeriana, and I was all set to start graduate school in February of the following year.

When they announced that Miss Venezuela was Vanessa Gonçalves, all I could think of was to say, "Ay chamo." You can see it clearly in that night's video. I thought I was talking to myself, but I said it out loud.

And I immediately asked myself, What now? What about my postgraduate degree; what about my efforts?

I struggled to hold back the tears; I was genuinely shocked. Instead of feeling happy, all I could think about was that everything I had built professionally was falling apart.

9.

Among the many myths that ran behind the backstage of Miss Venezuela, there was one that my boyfriend never tired of believing and repeating—that after the coronation, the winner was taken to a hotel where she was expected by men who had paid for her.

It was crazy for him to believe that, but he did. It was his fear.

Overnight, the poor guy went from having a dentist girlfriend who made his meals to being the boyfriend of a Miss Venezuela who didn't have a minute for him and was surrounded by another world. I saw that boyfriend mainly as my savior, the only one who had accepted me with all the widowhood story, the one I would probably marry. He said he stood by me, but he really didn't, and everything I was going through threw him off.

Today I laugh when I remember that, after the event was over, there was a photo shoot; I greeted my family, and the organizers told me:

"Gather your things; you're moving to another hotel."

My tension dropped; I wondered if the omens would come true. I began to pray. To make matters worse, my cellphone had run out of battery, and I had no way of having my family know I was being moved to another hotel.

I was put in a room all to myself—I had previously shared it with Miss Merida—and I was absolutely terrified. There was nothing to indicate anything wrong could happen to me, that anyone would try to enter my room at midnight. Anyway, I slept with an ice pick in my hands. Nothing happened.

Not long after, I broke up with that boyfriend—he didn't believe in marriage; he had never told me that before, and for me, the relationship had nowhere to go. We're still very good friends to this day.

10.

The night of the pageant, I was so scared and exhausted—I had been barely sleeping for days, attending continuous commitments—that I didn't have time to stop and think about what was happening to me, what it meant to have won the Miss Venezuela crown. I remember I gave thanks and fell asleep saying:

"My God, please give me the strength and the will to face what is coming."

The next day, I had a mixture of emotions. On the one hand, I was nervous and happy; on the other, sad and melancholic. It was hard to understand that all that excitement would be momentary, even if I were to win Miss Universe.

That moment was the beginning of the hardest stage.

I was in the eye of the hurricane with all eyes set on me, overloaded with activities and commitments. I was not prepared to lose my privacy and control over my time. I was not ready to be closely monitored about what I ate, how I dressed or put on my makeup, what I should say, my every move, my whole life. Nor had I imagined what it was like to not be able to eat with my parents without someone coming up to me, asking to take my picture. And I had to do it, to be nice; in the end, it was a kind gesture they were having toward me; no one was to blame for my contradictions.

Being Miss Venezuela was a twenty-four-hours-a-day, seven-days-a-week job. I had a lot of activities of social responsibility and advertising campaigns. In addition, I had to prepare for Miss Universe. Everything simultaneous, without respite. I attended intensive classes on make-up, public speaking, catwalk, theater, massages, training. Everything much more intensive than for Miss Venezuela.

As part of my responsibilities, I visited social and health institutions: San Juan de Dios Hospital, J.M. de Los Rios Hospital, and the Children's Orthopedic Hospital. Most significantly, I participated as a volunteer dentist in sessions of the NGO Operation Smile Venezuela, which took place nationwide that year. I had the opportunity to collaborate in some surgical interventions on craniofacial malformation lesions, especially cleft lip or palate. All of this was, of course, together with the medical team of the organization. It was, without doubt, one of my most satisfying activities as Miss Venezuela; it was a way to be a dentist again.

I also spent three weeks as co-host of the television program *Portadas* on the Venevisión channel. And I acted in the play *Don Quixote de la Mancha for children*, written and directed by José Rafael Briceño and staged by AGO Teatro en Escena 8 for the benefit of the Medatia Foundation. It was Briceño's idea for me to play the role of Dulcinea del Toboso; it was another way to prepare myself and strengthen my expressiveness. I had never done theater before.

11.

I went close to dropping out of Miss Universe.

Weeks after returning from Maracaibo, my aunt Mariette, my mother's older sister, fell sick. I was her favorite niece, and she was my favorite aunt, my friend, my confidant. We were very much alike, physically and in character. We were even born on the same date: February 10, both Aquarians.

What started out as lung cancer very quickly turned into a brain tumor and metastasis, against which months of chemotherapy and radiotherapy were not enough.

She died two weeks before my trip to São Paulo.

I was devastated; it all happened too fast. We got a call to tell us she had been taken to a hospital in Valencia. When we arrived, she was intubated with a look of desperation and anguish I'll never forget. I remember uncovering her feet, and as I began to massage them, a tear rolled down her cheek. I knew she was listening to me, and I tried to be supportive and calm; I told her if she needed to leave, she could do it calmly, that we would watch over her daughters. A few hours later, when we were at the hotel, we were notified that she had passed away.

The family was in shock. At that moment, I held back the tears and the anger. Someone had to be strong for the paperwork, and that was me. Afterward, I did break down. I was very affected; I called Osmel Sousa's assistant, Harry Levy, to tell him that I could not travel to São Paulo; I was emotionally destroyed. He convinced me to go on by telling me that I was already in the final stretch of the contest, that my aunt would not allow me to quit, so I went. I don't know where I got the strength.

12.

São Paulo, despite my state of mind, was an incredible experience.

Miss Universe was aired on September 12, 2011. I traveled a couple of weeks before for rehearsals and preparations.

The cultural exchange with the other 82 contestants was the most important thing. It's commonplace to say that, but it really was. Different ways of talking, eating, dressing, and seeing the world.

I remember one night, when all the girls were in the hotel lounge where we were meeting, I proposed a game, because I like nothing better than getting people to play. I asked them to have us listen to a song from each country and dance to it. They all ran to their phones. I played Reynaldo Armas' *Mi amigo el camino*. It's a song that immediately takes me back to my dad's restaurant. He always asked for Venezuelan music to be played in the mornings, and one day an employee, fed up with the same playlist, took out a CD and told me: "You're gonna love this song." And I did. That piece of music brings with it the smell of coffee, of empanada, of arepa, of a bright day:

My friend the road also gave me his comfort.

And told me never to cry

On the night of the event, Credicard Hall in São Paulo was aflame with excitement. There were millions of people from all over the world watching Miss Universe on television. When Venezuela was mentioned, there was a huge cheer that reminded me of soccer and baseball games at the university stadium.

Wearing the Venezuelan sash was a great pride and an immense responsibility. I was participating two years after one Venezuelan had handed the crown to another—Dayana Mendoza to Estefania Fernandez—and that, of course, was not well regarded among the other countries and generated additional pressure. To make matters worse, the previous year's Venezuelan representative had not been very disciplined in terms of schedules, and I paid the consequences— if an event was at nine in the morning, I was told it was at seven. It took me three days to realize what was happening. I complained to the chaperone, and he warned me that he had the order to always set appointments for me two hours earlier "because Venezuela's irresponsible." I had to tell him about my age and my commitment to the situation. They left me alone, and I never failed.

13.

I traveled all alone, with six suitcases and a box of my own size containing the typical costume, designed by Nidal Nouaihed and inspired by the Goddess Yara, an indigenous princess, queen of nature and love. The costume was very popular; it was an ecological cry for the sake of the planet. That goddess, I read later, was a sad woman with big green eyes, a bit like me.

In that truckload of luggage—the rest of the Misses had only two suitcases—there were clothes for every occasion that could come my way so that I would never use an outfit twice. Before leaving Caracas, the Miss Venezuela organization gave me a book with photographs of each garment, each shoe, and each piece of jewelry, plus instructions on how to combine them. I could not deviate from what was stipulated in that book; it was sacred law. I also carried an infinite number of products to do my hair and make-up. Venezuela was still a symbol of abundance, and my luggage sure was proof of it.

I remember, not without a tad of sadness, that one day, Miss Philippines knocked on the door of my room, desperately crying because she had lost a false eyelash. She had been given only one pair for the whole trip, and I had hundreds of them, a pair for every hour of the day, to change them as often as I wanted. Of course, I didn't hesitate to give her several packs.

On another occasion, my roommate, Miss Spain, was worried because she had no dress for an unscheduled event. I was carrying a lot of clothes I was not going to wear, and without even thinking about it, I lent her a dress. That night, as soon as I got back to the room, I got a call from Venezuela asking me why Miss Spain was wearing my clothes. I don't know how they found out. There were complaints and scolding. But I had done the right thing. Meanness is one of the things I hate the most.

I have a thousand anecdotes from those days in Brazil.

The food was terrible, almost all junk food, with lots of carbohydrates. Although I used to eat any kind of food without worrying, I couldn't afford to change my healthy diet, so one day I asked a security guard to sneak to the market and buy me some cans of tuna. At meals, I'd try to select vegetables, and as soon as I got to the room, I'd devour the tuna in its own can. I also did a bit of weight training because in those weeks in São Paulo, we didn't have the opportunity to go to the gym. I had brought some weights with me just in anticipation of that. Miss Spain used to tease me: "You do have willpower." It was willpower, but most of all, it was the awareness that being there and looking good was my job.

14.

The night before the Miss Universe pageant, we all had to showcase the evening gown we would wear. My gold and silver dress, designed by Gionni Straccia, had some transparencies the organizers didn't like and demanded to modify.

There was no time to look for another dress; I had no other dress for such an occasion. It was a holiday, and there were no seamstresses.

A real catastrophe.

Osmel Sousa, who was already in São Paulo, made a fuss about the incident, but knowing the impasse had to be solved somehow, he asked me if I had any flesh-colored or beige suit; he made me look for it, and I don't know where he found a seamstress, but he paid her a lot of money to make a sort of lining for the dress. From a distance, you couldn't tell it wasn't my skin.

Over the years, I have reviewed everything that happened in São Paulo, and I have come to understand that the pageant, for various reasons, but above all political ones, didn't have any qualms about making my life impossible. In a rehearsal, I felt bad because I hadn't eaten and they had the nerve of taking me to the infirmary to take a pregnancy test amid threats that if I was pregnant, I would have to leave the contest immediately. They were playing at wearing me out by attrition because they didn't want Venezuela to be among the finalists under any circumstances, let alone win the crown. Relations between Venezuela and the United States were already going through sour moments, and since Donald Trump was the owner of the contest, it all fell on me.

In spite of everything, the press insisted that I was at the top of the list of favorites.

I was very well placed in the preliminary competition—runway shows which included swimsuit, evening gown, and typical costume—with the highest score in my yellow bikini, which is why for a long while, I was called *La 9.1*. I was also among the frontrunners in the cybernaut votes through the contest website. I was selected among the sixteen finalists. For me, it was enough; my aspiration wasn't even to win Miss Venezuela, and

I had already gone too far. Besides, I had understood, by the contemptuous way I was treated, how the story would end.

As soon as the Miss Universe flashes were over, Osmel Sousa invited me to have dinner with my family in one of the hotel restaurants. When the waiter went to take my order, Osmel didn't let me speak and ordered a pizza for me. It was his way of telling me that the slavery of food was finally over. He told my parents I had done everything perfectly, that there was no doubt in his mind that I could have won, but there were reasons that had nothing to do with me. The next day I received calls from Joaquín Riviera and Venevisión executives to tell me the same thing.

Upon returning to Caracas, I was overcome by a deep melancholy, a feeling of emptiness; I had repressed all the sadness and mourning for my aunt's death. My career as a dentist was on standby, and I had to think again about what to do and where to go.

The night I handed the crown to the next Miss Venezuela, on October 15, 2011, I felt a little sadness, but most of all, I felt deeply relieved.

Another life was about to begin.

Tristeza Não Tem Fim, Felicidade Sim[1]

---

[1] *Sadness has no end; happiness does.*

1.

With the hustle and bustle of Miss Universe over, I was trying to get my priorities straight in order to return to the private practice of dentistry when proposals for corporate work began to appear.

I had never thought about it before.

First, a public institution called me to take care of their dental department. I turned it down because the conditions implied going to political marches and wearing the color of the ruling party.

Then an international business consultant contacted me to offer me a job as a dentist in a Venezuelan children's non-profit foundation, which in turn worked with other humanitarian organizations. I accepted because it suited my social interests, and it was a part-time job that allowed me to do other things, although we traveled through the country a lot. My work was simple— diagnostic and referral to specialists. I was there for about two years. I know perfectly well that I was hired because of the convenient image I provided by having been Miss Venezuela, not precisely because my profession was valued. I also knew, through other pageant contestants, that these kinds of situations, even absurd proposals, were commonplace, with tempting salaries but only betting on the physical shell.

At the same time, many ad campaigns started appearing which I couldn't refuse. It ended up taking me away from dentistry.

I worked with a brand of jeans made in Venezuela whose photographic production was all done in Colombia. I traveled a lot to Bogota. Those ironies of fate: I went to Bogota but not to begin my long-awaited graduate studies.

In 2012, I was *Chica Polar*, as models who promote one of the brands of Cervecería Polar are known; this is one of the most traditional brands in Venezuela, founded in the forties of the twentieth century

So, fashion shows and campaigns for different brands continued to appear, and not just Venezuelan ones. I traveled a lot, I didn't stop. I had offers to do soap operas, but I didn't dare. They proposed me to be a runway model; I didn't dare either. They talked about me as a sought-after model; that never ceased to surprise me and flattered me, but it made me more uncomfortable.

2.

One Sunday morning, my life took a 180-degree turn.

I was doing some running in the El Hatillo neighborhood when I ran into a spectacular man, a gorgeous actor I had seen on TV and who, like me, was into marathons.

I thought I'd faint.

He passed me and suddenly stopped and called out to me:

"Flaca[2]..."

I turned around:

"How are you, Vanessa Andrea?"

Nobody called me by my middle name. I fell for him.

He's the only boyfriend I've ever had who came from the so-called "show business."

Six months into our relationship, he had to move to Miami to do a soap opera. We spent four

---

[2] *Flaca:* Skinny one.

months going back and forth—an airport love affair between Caracas and Miami.

When I least expected it, he announced his plan was to stay in Miami, where he had better opportunities. He didn't want to go back to Venezuela.

"What about me?" I asked.

He asked me to live with him.

I was terrified of my parents' reaction. This was about me leaving the country, living with a man without getting married, arriving in an unknown city and country, leaving my job. At first, I didn't accept; then, he traveled to Caracas to talk to my dad about his intentions.

I left everything. Everything.

I left what had been my life to go to Miami with him.

It would not be the last time I would turn my life upside down in the pursuit of love.

3.

The first thing I did when I arrived in Miami was to enroll in an English course. My knowledge of the language was minimal, acquired in school. It was also the logical way to get a student visa, which later allowed me to apply for an O-1 non-immigrant visa designed for people with extraordinary abilities. Having participated in Miss Universe helped me a lot, as did my brief modeling career and my college profession.

It was a fresh start in everything.

Since we didn't have a car, I went to the course by bus. One day I was late for my class, and I said to myself: "It's only five miles; if you run that far, you can walk." So I set off. I had not taken the precaution of checking the weather—which you never do in Venezuela; I was not used to it—and then rain started pouring. I was soaking and cold.

I sat on the sidewalk and cried and cried.

4.

Suddenly, one day, he said he wanted to return to Venezuela because he wasn't achieving the success he had sought in Miami. Meanwhile, I was in the middle of the visa process; I couldn't leave the United States.

His work crisis coincided with our crisis as a couple, which was on the rise and had its share of infidelity issues on his part. He wanted me to drop my immigration process right there and go back to square one to be with him again, but I didn't. He left; I stayed, even though I knew it would be hard.

I stayed by myself. Alone by myself.

I knew no one in Miami. I had no friends of my own but his, no one to call when I got a flat tire on my car, no one to ask for help assembling furniture. No one to ask, somewhat embarrassed, how to fill my tank at gas stations that were so different from those in my country, where there was always someone to help you.

It was the first time I lived alone. I was living by myself and far away.

Living in a country that wasn't my own made everything more difficult at first.

I missed my family a lot. I missed my life, I missed everything.

I had sacrificed a lot of things; I did everything in my power to make the relationship work.

I had a very rough time in those early days.

He and I had shared the rent for the apartment, and overnight I had to take care of all the expenses on my own. I was able to keep paying for a few months; those were different times; renting an apartment required a lot of documents and money, none of which I had.

I spent a month living in hotels, jumping from one to another with my things and my bicycle in tow. Feeling frustrated, stranded, lost.

I was full of fears. I nullified my feelings, my goals, my desires. I nullified myself as a human being.

Fortunately, some Venezuelan friends had moved to Miami and took me in while my heart and finances stabilized.

Sadness took hold of me once again, almost paralyzing me.

But I didn't paralyze. During that time, I worked from sunup to sundown to support myself. I didn't yet have a residence. First, I was in a door-to-door shipping company, doing packaging and sticking labels. I worked in the warehouse Monday to Monday without air conditioning in the middle of summer. It was physically very exhausting; the boxes were heavy. I ended up with a shattered back, but I'll always be grateful to the Venezuelan businessman who gave me that opportunity.

Then I worked as an Uber driver. I had a driver's license, and at that time, it was very easy to subscribe to the app. It was great: I was earning good money and could manage my time to keep working out and doing whatever I wanted.

Quite a few times, I had to tell myself, repeating my dad's words: "Patience, this is the life of an immigrant, and it was the life of your father and grandparents. Patience, better times will come. Patience, this is your place, and here is where you have to persevere".

I can't be grateful enough for that failed love relationship, its sadness and bitterness, because it brought me where I am today—I emigrated, I made an effort, I managed to center myself. Now everything seems related and makes sense. Probably without that stumble of the heart, I wouldn't have left my country.

I also owe my second great depression to those moments.

5.

My goal was still to revalidate my dental degree, but it cost a fortune. The most expeditious option that would allow me to pursue my career was as a Dental Assistant with Expanded Functions course. I took it at the American Medical and Dental Institute.

I started working at the clinic of a colleague who had graduated before me in Caracas and was settled in Miami. My duties as an assistant were very restricted; they were literally those of an assistant, as stipulated by the health care system. I, once the master of my own practice, who got to do complex procedures, was on the sidelines of others, limited.

Despite feeling so uncomfortable, I continued as an assistant and managed to financially recover a little. I even managed to buy a small apartment.

With no ulterior motives, I quite often recommended the girl who had helped me find my apartment. Many Venezuelans bought or rented properties through her.

We became good friends.

One night in December 2015, she invited me to dinner, handed me a card, and with it, a considerable sum of money. It was her way of thanking me for the clients I had introduced her to. And she asked:

"Have you ever thought about getting your real estate sales agent license?"

I had never thought about it.

Never, until that very moment.

6.

A brief, intensive course turned me into a Real Estate Sales Agent for the State of Florida. Another unexpected change in my life that I welcomed with a jumble of emotions and insecurities.

Did I like it? No.

I needed the money, and I put my heart and soul into my new profession. I put everything into it, and the truth is, I did very well. I managed to buy an affordable apartment in a way I could never have imagined. It was a time of a real estate boom: Venezuelan migration was growing, and I needed properties.

That job led me to build, in a way, another fiction of myself.

I had to attend to a very active social life that was in total contradiction with my way of being. I had to dress, make up and wear heels every day. Real Estate is a form of seduction, and I had to undertake it with mastery.

Since the beginning, I worked at the most reputable real estate brokerage firms in Miami: Dora Puig's Luxe Living Realty and One Sothebys. With all of them, I learned a lot and immersed myself in a new world.

I felt compelled to take a course on sales skills because my knowledge as a salesperson was limited, even minimal. I thought I had the skills to listen to people, to understand their needs, but not to sell them something beyond their expectations. I was incapable of selling products I hadn't tried myself; it didn't convince me, and it didn't work in real estate either. So I landed at Harvard University in Cambridge, Massachusetts, to study Negotiation Skills. The experience was very stimulating. I participated together with very prominent people from the business world. Listening to them, learning how they developed their proposals, and how they executed sales was very important. I gained a lot of information.

It took some time for me to understand the magnitude of the learning I had taken in. I found the course content overwhelming at first; today it's very helpful. I've always been very grateful for what I've been able to learn, for the curiosity I feel to learn, and I do it with humility, acknowledging that I know nothing, that I can learn from a lot from people who may not have gone to Harvard but who have had significant experiences.

The real estate business, like Miss Venezuela before, took me out of my bubble, showed me other scenarios of reality, almost all very hard, not exempt from competition, rudeness, drugs. I had been overprotected, my contact with drugs very distant, as a simple spectator. I had to take care of myself. I had to fit into this new cosmos without ceasing to be myself.

At the same time, modeling campaigns and advertising events continued to show up. I led a life in my own way, with certain luxuries and comfort. I was a minor celebrity in Venezuela and in Miami. It didn't bother me. But none of that changed me on the inside; nothing obscured my essence.

7.

My heart still lay bare. Wounded.

One day, a friend I had when I was Miss Venezuela reappeared.

I didn't recognize him. I remembered him as very fat, and he wasn't anymore.

We started dating, we became a couple. He was very attentive to me.

When we had been dating for about four months, one of his trips coincided with Mother's Day, and I asked him to give me a contact in order to send a bouquet of flowers to my mother. The bouquet arrived, and it was beautiful. My mom was thrilled; she sent me a picture, and I forwarded it to him with my thanks.

Minutes later, I received a message from his Whatsapp:

"Why are you writing to my husband?"

And then a picture of him in a disheveled bed, sleeping.

In shock, I clarified very politely that I understood they had separated and that if they were trying to rebuild their marriage, I would move away. She replied:

"I'm not his daughter's mother; I am his wife of eight years."

I couldn't believe this was happening to me.

Then he called again and again. When I finally answered, he apologized and then explained it was an old girlfriend he had in Caracas.

Even though I broke up with him and asked him to stay away, when he returned to Miami, he started communicating again, sending me gifts. He apologized, said I was the woman of his life, said I should give him another chance.

For more than six months, he continued courting me and trying to show he was sincerely sorry. He was very attentive; that flattered me. Very much against what I now know I won't forgive, non-negotiably—infidelity— I forgave him, and we got back together.

Today I can recognize and understand this was my first toxic relationship, to which I became attached because of my need to feel protected, surrounded by lies, conflicts, and constant problems.

Now I understand I was in a relationship with a narcissist. I used to think this term applied to a person who takes care of his appearance, but it's really about a behavioral disorder that acts by manipulation, that detects what another person likes, her lacks and needs in order to seduce her, creating a dependent relationship.

It was three years surrounded by conflicts, attentions, infidelities, flattery, lies, trips, deceit. A constant roller coaster of emotions that greatly affected my self-esteem and my confidence as a woman. It was hard for me to leave that relationship and realize that, even though I can now be grateful for the way it helped me, it was a very harmful one.

I was searching for love, real love. I was searching for it anxiously, as before, as always.

AND SHE HEARD THE VOICE OF GOD IN A BLIND WELL

1.

One Saturday morning, like so many others, I
went out to do my cycling routine.

Before that, I called a friend, Javi. I asked him
if he'd be in the area where we used to ride; he said
yes. Then we would have coffee together.

"Ok, see you," I said.

That day I decided I would speed-train because
I needed to push myself a bit harder.

I was pedaling very well, with a lot of strength.
I had done three laps. I used to do between four
and five. In front of me, there was a group of guys.
I didn't want to lose my speed, so I asked them:

"Lefty please."

They did indeed pull to the side, and I passed
them. But I immediately heard them agree to
increase their speed to catch up with me. I was no
stranger to that macho, competitive spirit.

I turned to see how close they were to me.

And that's the last I remember.

2.

I woke up hours later in the hospital with a bunch of wires in my chest and my hands in pain, stained with blood. There were several doctors around me, watching.

"What am I doing here?" I asked in dismay.

I immediately saw my friend, who fortunately found me passed out on the asphalt next to a guy who was calling 911 and then disappeared without explaining what had happened. I can guess someone brushed against one of my wheels and made me lose my balance, and then the whole group fled in fear of police interrogation.

"Relax, you're fine," said my friend.

He told me that, in the ambulance taking me to the hospital, I woke up, and when the paramedics questioned me, I was able to give my first and last name, but when they asked for my address, I readily gave the one from Caracas. There was no way I could give them my Miami address. I don't know why my mind went so far away and clung to home, where I had lived in Caracas, my parents' home.

Once in the emergency room, my friend asked who in my family to call. I told him a cousin for the moment; I didn't want my parents to find out.

They did CT scans and other tests on me. I had a fracture of the skull's temporal bone, which protects the left lobe of the brain, the cranial nerves, and the middle and inner ears.

I was hospitalized for four days.

For two days, I was able to hide from my mother, but on the third day, she called very worried:

"Vanessa Andrea, I want to hear your voice and see you. Please answer."

Mothers know so much; they have an unbeatable intuition.

I told her, tried to reassure her. Distance, in cases like this, is harder than ever. Nothing I said would be enough to make her stop worrying. It distressed me that my parents would be distressed for me.

The doctor explained that I was lucky the helmet was of good quality because the blow was so hard that it had broken anyway. The fracture hadn't been fatal by just a few millimeters.

3.

Because of that fall, I lost eighty percent of the hearing in my left ear. Also, since that event, I have suffered from tinnitus, an unbearable noise. They said it would disappear when the inflammation went down.

I went to many doctors.

At first, I stopped all my activities hoping that the buzzing that disturbed me would stop. It never did. In addition, initially, I felt a lot of confusion, dizzy spells, and headaches.

I had to learn to live with tinnitus, with my deafness. I had to adapt to my noises and silences to make them part of my life. Sometimes we don't realize how resilient we are, how much we're able to adapt to even the most terrible things. Human beings always learn to dance in their own discomfort.

No one has ever said my deafness is a disability, but it is. It has led me to pay close attention to the lips of those who speak to me, especially in noisy places. If I'm with people I trust, I ask them to stand on my right side because if they're on my left, I have to turn my head.

Learning to navigate with deafness has made me be more and more present.

Not hearing one hundred percent has helped me to listen more to people, and better too, to pay more attention to them, to listen with the heart. This ability to listen differently is a blessing; I have no doubt.

FOR STRONG AS DEATH IS LOVE

1.

The purchase of a gift for a christening led me again to burn ships.

That story was long and began with the mundane fact of going to a jewelry store. There was a young man there who had been very serious, distant to me up to that moment. This time, he was very kind and friendly.

Soon after, he started following me on Instagram, leaving me flattering, flirtatious messages, and he wrote to me worried when he saw photos in which I appeared with my hand in a cast—three months after the bicycle fall, I had accepted an invitation to practice Stand Up Jet Ski, a very light and fast personal jet ski that requires a lot of concentration and balance. When I got on a platform, the bike went flying on one side and I went flying on the other, with the bike falling on my left hand. I broke three fingers, and they told me I had to give up risky sports for a while.

The accident made us start writing to each other every day, always through Instagram. It was much later when he asked for my phone number.

And one day, he invited me to dinner.

With the first words we exchanged, I felt a connection, as if we had known each other all our lives or from another life. It was inexplicable. Everything he said came naturally to me.

At another dinner later on, he asked about a bracelet I was wearing. I told him it was the figure of St. Benedict, that I had been raised in a Catholic family, that in Miami I attended a prayer group that helped me a lot. He insisted on something I already knew:

"I'm Jewish."

I told him that in my quests I had attended Kabbalah classes, that I knew something of his religion.

He emphasized he was not an observant Jew.

2.

We started seeing each other frequently. We began dating. We had a relationship.

One day, he asked me for help moving the jewelry store into a new location within the same mall; I gladly went. It was there that I saw his mother for the first time. He introduced me as his girlfriend.

At the end of the relocation, he dismissed me by saying he had to go to dinner alone with his mother. Weird.

The next day, he invited me to dinner, and without much preamble, he blurted out:

"Do you know that if I wanted to marry you, you'd have to convert to Judaism?"

In a few words, he explained to me it was the only way for our future children to be Jewish, which was very important to him. I was not afraid of the subject. I understood perfectly well that Judaism is an inheritance only transmitted when you are born from a Jewish womb, that becoming Jewish was the only way to solve this identity issue.

I found it curious that, not being a religious man, he had such a requirement from me. In fact, he not only wasn't a churchgoer: he never participated in the family rites.

One Friday, his brother—who had become increasingly orthodox—was going to his father's house for Shabbat, and I asked why didn't we all go. My boyfriend refused; I understood then that all the problems and the distance he had from his family were precisely due to their differences regarding religion.

As I always do when a subject matters to me, I got a bibliography and began studying Jewish rituals and traditions.

I went to a kosher market one Friday and bought everything I needed for a Sephardic Shabbat dinner, just like the one at his home, and I surprised him. It was the first time Shabbat had been celebrated in his own home. I googled the phonetic version of the Friday prayers; he did the Kiddush and I did the candles.

Thus began my journey to Judaism.

My only purpose was to make him feel comfortable, to smooth things out with his family because I knew it caused him pain.

My interest grew and became very genuine. I wanted to learn more, read more, to know in depth the reason for the rites, the history of the traditions. I would put into practice what I had learned, prepare other festivities; we would talk about subjects he hadn't touched since graduating from high school in Caracas. We would spend entire nights talking.

For me, everything was new and fascinating.

3.

There came a time when I wanted to go a step further, and I asked a friend if he knew someone who could give me classes on Judaism. I needed a structure; I needed my learning to be much deeper. I couldn't continue acquiring knowledge only through the Internet, in a self-taught way. I was doing it because I was genuinely interested in it; it wasn't a question of conversion or a possible future together. We hadn't talked about it again.

My friend, surprised and believing that all that effort was useless, said to me:

"Don't get too excited about that relationship."

His advice broke my heart. I was sincerely confident this was the man of my life and Judaism a spiritual path I had discovered for my own good. I was full of doubts, hungry for knowledge.

So, I arrived at a rabbi's office, and the first thing he said was:

"You want to convert. You have a Jewish boyfriend and you want to convert..."

It was hard for me to make him understand these were not my reasons and intentions.

Soon, Sunday classes began at three o'clock in the afternoon. I also went to a Shabbat ceremony that I found very beautiful because they sang and played accordion. Everyone had arrived in their cars, and they wouldn't turn off their cell phones during the ceremony.

My boyfriend knew nothing about these incursions. When I told him about it, he flipped—I'd been attending a Reform synagogue, which did everything his family saw as forbidden and sinful.

"If your wishes are serious, I'll take you to my rabbi," he said.

That rabbi's wife offered the classes I really needed. She was a very kind rabbanit to me and is still my friend to this day. They are orthodox, super orthodox.

They also asked:

"Why do you want to study our religion? Are you really not just looking for conversion in order to get married?"

4.

At first, I had classes twice a week, then three times a week. I also went to the synagogue on Fridays.

I remember the first Friday I asked a friend to go with me. He didn't want to; he was very distant from his Judaism. We received some weird looks. When they asked about my last name, doubt arose about whether to let me in or not. I remember I made that friend stand in the middle of the street with some rabbis who were wearing tefillin, or phylacteries —little boxes containing holy scriptures, placed on the arm and head—. He hadn't done that since his Bar Mitzvah. I would have loved to be a man and wear them.

Maybe in another life, I was a Jewish man, and that's why it all comes so naturally to me.

Several people around me reconnected with their Judaism through my efforts, even my boyfriend. That makes me proud. I find it beautiful, touching; it makes me happy.

As I became more involved with Judaism, it became mandatory for my boyfriend to allow me to engage with his family.

That was the beginning of a little big tragedy.

His parents were divorced. His mother was living in Venezuela at the time and didn't seem to have a problem with our relationship. However, every time she traveled to Miami and I suggested having a Shabbat at our house, I was met with excuses. He'd say the situation with his mother was complicated, problematic. Only later would I understand why.

His father accepted me half-heartedly, but for his second wife—who had converted in order to marry, by the way—I was a threat. She barely complied with some precepts, and I was the proof that much more could be done. During the first Shabbat with them, she, annoyed, asked me:

"Why are you making all these changes in your life? Why?"

My rule of life is to do things right. Give it all I've got. Overexert myself, even. With Judaism, it wasn't going to be any other way. Everything I learned, I applied. I was so involved that I took care of all the details; I knew all the blessings, the songs, what to eat or not to eat. I think I was overshadowing other women converts, and they resented it. Besides, the comparisons began; it was inevitable. I, at heart, wasn't looking for any ostentation. I was being myself.

I was becoming an uncomfortable element for many other women in the Jewish community as well.

Later, my boyfriend would explain to me that his parents had divorced so that his father could marry that lady, who eventually converted to Judaism by simple social protocol and in a not very orthodox way, as I could have done. That generated deep discomfort in the family, and I wound up paying the consequences. I didn't know anything about that; I found out when our relationship was well underway. Besides, he told me his father had never bet on our relationship and now was in shock, while his mother demanded a formal conversion process if we wanted to go on.

"Whatever needs to be done, I'll do it; I'm already doing it," I told him.

He seemed to be delighted with my process. He kept telling me I made him happy, that he wanted me to be the mother of his children, that he was sure I would lead a Jewish home. He said he admired my passion, that he wanted to marry me, that I was ideal for him.

For me, it was the perfect story.

He trusted the words of the Song of Songs: "I am for my beloved, and my beloved is for me."

5.

My garments had to be adapted to the requirements of *tzniut* (Hebrew for modesty). This has to do with discretion and modesty, with subtracting attention from the body so that it doesn't distract, in such a way that we value it and don't look at it superficially. Thus, torso, thighs, calves, forearms, chest, areas near the neck, and hair, in the case of married women, can't be seen.

Little by little, I changed my outfits. I wore long skirts, long-sleeved blouses, closed collars. I went to the gym and to yoga with those excessive and uncomfortable clothes, even in the Miami heat, even at the beach, where I could never wear a bathing suit again. I always tried to combine my diet, my exercises, and my life with that new life, which could be natural in Israel, but not in Miami.

Things became more and more complicated.

I wasn't aware of all the obstacles his family was creating. He hid them so as not to make me suffer. His mother was against us, and so were his

142

siblings. In fact, his mother demanded that he leave me because all she asked of her children was that they marry a Jewish woman. He was desperate, but even then, he was confident we'd get through it.

One day he remarked, a bit on the fly, that his older brother had said that if we didn't want our children to suffer in the future because I was a convert, the only conversion the family would admit to would have to be carried out in Israel.

The pressure exerted by the mother was such that everything became muddled and we decided to end the relationship, which had become increasingly distant from love and ended up wrapped up in thick, confusing, and painful issues.

I became pure sadness.

However, I wanted to finish what I had started. My conversion was beyond marriage. I identified with Judaism, so I resolved to go to Israel anyway and see what it was all about. It would only be fifteen days that would distance me a little from the pain.

6.

When I arrived in Jerusalem, I felt like I was almost naked.

The tzniut clothes I had been wearing in Miami were inappropriate.

The school where I went to study was located inside the Old City, in the Jewish Quarter. It was an orthodox area. You had to cover your hair; there couldn't even be a glimpse of your ankle.

I remember one morning we agreed with the rabbanit to go shopping for books. I wore a brown skirt below the knee, a long-sleeved white blouse with buttons down the front, and my hair down. We all went into the bookstore—most of us were Latin Americans in the process of converting—and when I was finished, I went out and sat down in a small square. Suddenly a woman in a building started shouting in Hebrew. I couldn't understand a thing. Someone translated for me—all that fuss was about me because I was showing part of my legs and chest. She said I was there to tempt the men in the neighborhood.

The next day I had to wear opaque stockings, long skirt, closed blouse, hide my hair. It was summer; the heat was unbearable.

However, nothing disturbed me. The classes were fascinating. I felt immersed in a destiny. Walking through the streets of the old city of Jerusalem was an indescribable experience. The Shabbat ceremony was beautiful. I loved everything I was seeing: the values, the humility, a sense of family that connected me very much with my own Portuguese family. Everyone there had many children, as I dreamed, and they took care of each other. They all collaborated to make the Shabbat rite perfect, a refuge. They shared the food at a very long table.

It was another reality.

It was like making up for all the shortcomings I had experienced in the United States, all my loneliness and sadness. It was very gratifying; I identified with everything; I felt this was precisely what I had been looking for. I felt at home, as if I had been there before, as if I had always walked those cobblestone streets, those corners full of history. I felt everything was immensely vast, sacred, and perfect.

While I was there, he called me.

He couldn't believe I had gone to Israel without him, in spite of him.

7.

I returned to Miami very excited, eager to rush my return to Jerusalem and stay for the other three months that were supposedly needed to complete my conversion.

I arranged everything for my return.

In the meantime, I met with him, who suddenly wanted to come back with me.

"When you finish the conversion, I'm sure my family will accept you," he said.

One day we went out to lunch with his dad, and he was full of praise for what I was doing. He told us we had his support.

My intention wasn't to restart the relationship. I had kept doing all that because I needed to, because I honestly felt it was my path.

8.

As soon as I was back in Jerusalem, a thousand problems erupted.

I wasn't allowed to stay in the schoolhouse inside the Old City; I had to stay with a Colombian lady and her daughter, who were in the same process as me and lived in a relatively nearby area. I lived a thoroughly humble life there. The shower was so small I couldn't stretch my arms. I slept on a mattress on the floor, for a while in the company of rats we couldn't get rid of. I owe a lot to her, Esther. We still keep in touch. She says I'm her premium daughter and always lights a candle for me.

Later, the rabbanit explained to me that "someone" had shown them pictures and videos of when I worked in advertisement and was Miss Venezuela. I explained to them this wasn't me anymore.

They also said the conversion wouldn't take three months but one more. There were a thousand excuses that I still didn't understand.

In any case, I was living a very interesting experience in every sense, from the spiritual to the most everyday things. I could tell a thousand stories and sensations about those days in the Holy Land.

One morning, on my way back from the market, the bus didn't stop at my bus stop and drove on. When I finally managed to get off with my shopping cart, I walked along what I thought was the edge of the wall, close to where I lived.

Suddenly, I heard the muezzin and the chanting that summons Muslims to prayer. It was very close. Of course, I was in the middle of the Muslim Quarter and was wearing clearly Jewish clothes and, to top it off, a Star of David around my neck. I walked briskly, head down, knowing that I was passing through a bunch of men who looked at me and said things to me in Arabic. Suddenly one of them spat on my shoulder and started swearing at me in English. I kept rushing without looking up, terrified, praying.

I silently asked myself, "Vanessa, what are you doing here? What are you doing with your life?"

I came home crying. Esther was alarmed:

"Are you okay?" she asked me.

But I was not. I told her everything, and she said:

"That shows you what it means to be a Jew."

I am sure very few Jews I know have gone through situations as humiliating and degrading as the ones I experienced in Israel, where I felt I could have even been killed. I had never experienced such terrible harassment as a Portuguese, Venezuelan, or immigrant. And I understood why the Jewish culture is so closed and marked by mistrust.

In any case, Israelis are generally open, warm, very welcoming people. Outside the orthodox communities, they are very relaxed about religion. I met a number of tattooed young people who thought quite liberally regarding sexuality and society. That's what I saw, although my experience was taking place in an absolutely religious environment.

150

Apart from these and other incidents, I still felt very comfortable. I believed all the effort I was making to stay in Israel and achieve my conversion made sense. I felt the life I was leading, stripped of vanity, of material comforts, was part of my quest. I had stepped out of my comfort zone; I liked that. The family bonding I perceived was what I kept dreaming of for my own life.

9.

Much to my regret, I had to return to Miami without completing the conversion.

Everything was getting more and more hostile.

The three months it would take would be extended, and they wouldn't tell me how long or why. I had discovered that the "someone" who had shown my photos and talked about my life as Miss Venezuela had been my brother-in-law. My already ex-boyfriend's family apparently had a lot of influence, both in Israel and Miami, and moved heaven and earth to make everything difficult for me. They wanted me to give up and, of course, stay away from him.

This time I came back broken, disenchanted.

However, I believed I could still complete my conversion in Miami. Besides, I had resumed the relationship that had led me to that whole process, and this time it looked like we would make it to the chuppah, the Jewish wedding altar.

We visited a rabbi for guidance. Now it was no longer just about conversion but about getting married. More studies. More obstacles. He also had to study.

We had to undertake many other changes. No more sleeping together as we had been doing for the year and a half we had been dating. Not even holding hands, let alone kissing.

My life as an observant Jew was never easy In Miami. I was always looked at strangely; I didn't fit in. No matter how hard I tried, I felt rejected by Jews and non-Jews alike.

I came to understand a few things in a line at Starbucks. I was wearing a *tzniut,* and a man looked at me as no man had ever looked at me before: with a touch of compassion, but above all, with a deep look that, rather than piercing through all the layers of clothing I was wearing, looked at me as a human being, beyond the appearances provided by the clothes and the shapes of the body. I, coming from a world where overexposure of the body was the natural thing to do, where women are perceived as prey worthy of hunting, understood that a woman can be seen in another way, without prejudice, without clichés, without undressing.

And that became a law of life for me.

That's why my networks are not overflowing with obvious poses or insinuations that could very well bring me more followers and even job proposals, but that wouldn't reflect me as the person I am. I know perfectly well what sells and what doesn't, but I'm not interested in taking advantage of that. During the time I spent hiding my body, it allowed me to value it in its proper measure. Today, my yoga clothes show my body, but I feel comfortable, not different from other people.

10.

Shortly after returning from Israel, my first nephew was born in Barcelona, and I went to meet him. My parents traveled as well.

I kept dressing according to the precepts of *tzniut* and observing some Shabbat customs, so one Friday, I had my brother drop me off near a synagogue: I didn't want to be seen arriving by car. On the small staircase leading to the temple, I was asked a thousand questions. Again, my last name didn't make my presence there understandable, and besides, I had gone alone. However, they treated me kindly and invited me to the Shabbat dinner. Then I made my way back on foot. It was about two hours of walking, sometimes through very lonely streets. That night my brother questioned me:

"You're crazy. I guess you're clear that you're crazy. What's the point of all this? What are you doing with your life?"

The next day I went back to the synagogue. I went walking and came back the same way.

In Barcelona, I went to the kosher market and didn't eat what they prepared at my brother's. They would invite me to a restaurant and I'd go with them, but I wouldn't eat. My family treated me at that time and always with a lot of patience and respect, with great love. On one occasion, I even invited them to eat at a kosher restaurant, and not only did they accept but allowed themselves to enjoy the experience.

11.

Once again, the relationship ended despite all my efforts.

It wore out little by little and became tinged with very difficult, very unfair situations. He loved me, and I loved him. We'd never had an argument. He, like no one else so far, had respected and valued me.

But we couldn't be together. It was hopeless.

The family pressure became unbearable. There were put-downs, threats. I felt they were breaking me into a thousand pieces. Our relationship even made them threaten to kick him out of the commercial partnership where he worked.

And I didn't insist. I didn't want him to suffer more.

I chose to walk away. We cut short all we had lived together. It had to be this way so as not to hurt us anymore.

Everything I had longed for stopped making sense.

Thus began my third great depression.

12.

Getting my life back on track was challenging.

It took me a while to stop feeling guilty.

For a few months, I remained a *shomer Shabbat* (Sabbath-observant) until it became an insurmountable barrier to getting a job. It wasn't easy to make it understood that I couldn't work Friday afternoons, Saturdays, or specific dates during the year.

The comparison between what I experienced in Israel and my life in Miami made me somewhat humble and grateful. I remember the day I returned from Israel and used the shower at home: it seemed huge. It was strange to have hot water for as long as I wanted. During that first shower in Miami, I sat under the water to cry and, above all, to give thanks.

I wish I had understood at the moment that everything happens the way it's supposed to happen. That it had been an education, a growth process that would lead me to where I am today, where I feel comfortable, fulfilled, secure. That's why I stopped measuring the pain involved, the grief of love, the sacrifices.

"Don't let the plans you have for yourself be more important than yourself," says Wayne Dyer in *Your Erroneous Zones*, a book that marked me a lot.

Step by step, I stripped myself of some of the habits I had acquired and kept the ones that touched my heart the deepest because my identification with Judaism is still intact even today. Sometimes I do Shabbat, sometimes I keep some festivities. I can't forget phrases, prayers, teachings.

She, the girl who tried to be Jewish, is also me.

I kept the good, forgot the bad; I even stopped reproaching love relationships. I have no doubt that this experience led me to be more open-minded, to recognize, accept and understand cultural and religious differences, to be more tolerant and empathetic.

13.

Three sentences from the book *Man's Search for Meaning*, by Viktor Frankl, allowed me to take another look at what I was going through, and they continue to be a source of understanding for me today because I believe that love, that process, was an act of courage and survival:

"In some way, suffering ceases to be suffering at the moment it finds a meaning, such as the meaning of a sacrifice."

"Between the stimulus and response, there is a space. And in that space lies our freedom and power to choose our responses. In our response lies our growth and our freedom."

"When the impossibility of replacing a person is realized, it allows the responsibility which a man has for his existence and its continuance to appear in all its magnitude. A man who becomes conscious of the responsibility he bears toward a human being who affectionately waits for him, or to an unfinished work, will never be able to throw away his life. He knows the 'why' for his existence, and will be able to bear almost any 'how.'"

DEPRESSION: THE LUST OF DARKNESS

1.

Depression is a cold.

A fall into the void.

Suffocation, dizziness.

A very dark cloud approaching, enshrouding, engulfing.

2.

The first time I was depressed, I was fully aware I was. It was obvious. My first boyfriend had died tragically. It was too hard a blow, and it seemed a foregone conclusion that I wouldn't get over it without help.

I was still living with my parents, and my mom was the first to notice:

"Vanessa, I think you'd better go to a psychologist."

I had lost my appetite; I was terribly thin, with no strength at all. I stopped exercising, something so important to me even then. I spent whole days in bed, weekends in bed. I stopped reading, cooking, talking to people. I just wanted to sleep, to lie with my eyes closed. Seeing was painful; thinking hurt.

I was in therapy for about a year. It was a terrible year; the depression was very disabling. I could barely keep up with college. I was going from home to class and from class to home. It was very exhausting. I could hardly sustain enough concentration to study and see patients.

When I felt like taking up exercise again, I understood the dark cloud was moving away, that step by step, I was coming out of my depression and regaining my life.

At that moment, the psychologist recommended that instead of locking myself in a gym, I should be in contact with nature, breathing fresh air, so I began to climb the trails of El Avila mountain. At first, I did it as a hike with friends on Saturdays. Then it became a routine on Saturdays and Sundays, and later, I added other days of the week. At six in the morning, I would climb the mountain, return home, take a shower and fly to the university.

I climbed El Avila at least once a week until the last day I was in Caracas. It was a sacred, revitalizing routine.

3.

I ran into the face of depression again in Miami.

It was at the end of my relationship with my actor boyfriend.

One day I came home from the English course and found him packing the household goods into boxes. There was never a "this is yours, this is mine." We had bought everything together. It was a messy, painful, horrible breakup. We ended up dividing the tableware, the glasses, the pots and pans. We didn't split the mattress in two because it wasn't possible. Half and half everything. The house was falling apart, and so was my heart.

It was unexpected. I had left my life to be with him.

The cloud was reappearing. Pitch black. Like an immense storm.

The sadness returned, and with it, the lack of appetite, the listlessness, the need to stay in bed, to do nothing.

Everything was darkness around me. It was as if a switch in me had been turned off.

I stopped exercising, I stopped enjoying, I stopped living.

Fortunately, I still had some energy to seek help.

I started seeing the psychologist at the institute where I was studying English, the one that had previously detected my ADHD. She suggested I see a psychiatrist because my depression looked dangerous.

I went to several sessions with a lady of Cuban origin. For me, it's crucially important to empathize with people, feel comfortable with their gaze, their body attitude, with what I like to call their *energy*. And with her, there was not the slightest connection—she was somber, I would say heavy.

One day I arrived at her office and found a commotion. People were running from one office to another. Police inspectors showed up. My psychiatrist had committed suicide the day before. They were in the middle of an investigation, and there was me, with my depression.

From that clinic, I was referred to a psychiatrist who, almost as soon as he saw me, without saying many words, said:

"You have a severe depression; I'm going to prescribe you antidepressants."

I felt desperate, miserable. In the United States, they prescribe antidepressants too lightly. I have always shied away from medications that aren't strictly necessary, but I recognized I was depressed and admitted it. I couldn't afford to put my life on hold for a year; I was alone in Miami; I had to find a place to live, work, to stay on my feet.

Three months later, thinking I had recovered, feeling confident, I quit taking the medication, which made me feel agitated and gave me insomnia. I quit the wrong way, on my own and in one go. One day I threw the pills in the trash, which was ignorant and utterly irresponsible. You can't quit an antidepressant overnight, no matter how well you feel. It is absolutely counterproductive.

The cloud came back with bolts, thunder, and lightning. Blacker than ever.

I began to feel afraid. I didn't want to leave the house and couldn't, either. Fear was mixed with sadness. It was a disaster. My mind and body were a mess. Never before or since have I felt so out of control and out of my mind. I had no control over any emotion. I was going from sadness to fear, from exhaustion to acceleration. I was going crazy. I was working out like crazy. I could go out at six in the morning and run five miles, then swim, go to work and come back, take the bike, and then do weights. I didn't stop. I couldn't and didn't know how to stop. I slept for three hours if that.

The advantage I took from those complex days was that I concentrated on the world of triathlons and marathons. I participated in as many as I could. It was the only thing that brought me any joy. It was a way to channel the excess training I was doing. A way to escape from my life and from dissatisfaction.

I actually started participating in races in 2010, right after I was crowned Miss Venezuela. I was encouraged to do it by some swimming buddies at the Portuguese Center—I was looking for training apart from what I was getting at the gym—and thanks to them, I ran short races, three and five kilometers, which were very common at that time in Caracas.

My first ten-kilometer race was in El Hatillo, and soon after, I went to live in Miami, where I found plenty of options. I started there with short races until I reached the half marathon: I participated in several, including one on the beach sand. I also did a group relay race where each runner ran a stretch until we reached Key West. That's how I got to half marathons I ran in San Francisco, New York, and Puerto Rico. I incorporated cycling and was able to participate in triathlons and cycling races as well.

The body has limits.

I didn't listen when I said to myself, "Not today," "I can't do it anymore," or "I need to rest." That's why I had several injuries. It was like a self-punishment I was inflicting on myself: I felt stopping meant losing. Again, I believed I could not fail myself. I convinced myself the only way not to fall further into depression was by not giving up, running marathons, exhausting myself physically to the point of fainting.

And I was really exhausted; I couldn't take it anymore.

The depression, far from improving or fading with the extreme physical work, got worse.

4.

With much embarrassment, I went back to the psychiatrist. She told me what I already knew:

"You can't quit antidepressants overnight; you've done yourself great harm."

I wanted something to regulate me, to bring me back to self-awareness. I certainly had a lot of anxiety; I was short of breath. The doctor said it was panic attacks.

She prescribed milder pills that would allow me to gradually wean off the medication in a controlled and safe manner, as it should be.

It took me a year to get back to myself. The neurochemical imbalance I had self-generated had been profound.

Love failures and the remnants of depression at that time made me an even more insecure woman and led me to new wounds, to relationships with men who didn't value me. I was even in a relationship with someone who tried to physically abuse me; fortunately, I ran away just in time.

They did not value me, but neither did I value myself. I stayed in those relationships believing I deserved it. I played a bit of a victim, clinging to unhappiness.

Everything I admitted was part of my depression. Without realizing it, I was becoming more permissive. It wasn't normal; it wasn't right.

Meanwhile, life went on, and I thought life was the passing of one day and another and another, with its shocks and sadness, without peace.

5.

The most severe depression was the one I experienced when I returned from Israel and ended the relationship that almost had me converted to Judaism.

Amid my attempts at resuming my former activities, everything went dark again. The cloud covered everything. Lightning and fear returned. Although shorter than the others, this was the deepest one: never before had I had such negative thoughts, never before had I imagined myself in life-threatening situations.

It's not easy for me to admit it, but I thought a thousand times about suicide.

I wondered what was the point of it all, why go on living.

I came to glimpse ways to do it. I never got to plan it, but I could imagine it: I lived on a twenty-fifth floor, and I had no doubt that if I did it, it would be by throwing myself from that balcony. I worried that other options would leave me alive and in a worse situation than the one I was trying to escape.

I longed for a button that would turn me off completely, that there'd be no afterward. No more suffering. No more pain. No more thinking.

In those moments, I reviewed all my relationships, my failures, my bouts of sadness. I recriminated myself for many things; I punished myself. I walked in circles around myself; I felt victimized and out of control again. The only thing that kept me from taking a step further and ending my life was the thought of my family, who didn't deserve the tragedy I was about to create.

I had made many changes in my life to convert to Judaism, and not succeeding gave me a deep sense of failure. To throw it all away meant an emptiness. I was afraid again; I came to wonder if God would punish me for having found a path and not following it.

6.

As I take a last look at this book, I receive some heartbreaking news: a person very close to my family has committed suicide.

He tried the first time but was pulled out of it, saved. Two days later, he succeeded. He had a history of several suicides in his family and dealt with a wife who was always very depressed. But we never saw any behavior in him that would suggest the turmoil he carried inside. I can't imagine what he was going through that made him want to die, fail, not regret it and do it again. Life gave him a second chance, and he didn't take it. I once read that after every completed suicide, there are several attempts.

This made me think long and hard about why no one around him noticed he was depressed. I don't judge him or his family. I respect that suicide was his decision, but I can't help believing it could have been prevented, that it was an unattended problem.

Right now, I don't have the exact words to describe how much that death has affected me. It has impacted me in a way I couldn't have anticipated. I spent days in deep sadness. Mixed feelings were roiling in me. Seeing my family so distraught, heartbroken, and helpless took me back to those days when I had wanted to die myself.

It was like looking at myself in a mirror.

I could imagine my family in that tragedy, in great pain because of me.

Today I believe few people are genuinely aware of others; few actually listen when someone tells them their problems. Few are present and able to offer genuine comfort. The most usual responses when someone feels depressed are, "That's nothing," "It will pass," "There are worse problems in life," "You'll be fine." I've heard all of these myself, and those are not helpful answers; to you, what you're going through may seem like the end of the world, even if others think it's nonsense. No one said to me, "I understand you." Just "I understand; I can understand how you feel."

Every day I understand better and more clearly how important it is that we all have tools and can use them to overcome difficult moments so as to identify when someone close to us is suffering from depression. If there were more information, much suffering would be avoided. It is essential to know ourselves, not to underestimate our own and other people's problems, to be more aware of the processes we go through as human beings.

It's because of this story, which is my story and the story of many people I have known who at some point had the idea of suicide hovering around them, that I insist that vulnerability and empathy are so essential. We need to speak openly, without fear of the stigmatization that comes with the mental health issues that are so commonplace today. We all suffer from something; it is very human and characteristic of contemporary societies.

7.

My last depression was my teacher, my master's degree in the knowledge of myself as a being, as a person, of my behaviors and my evolution towards a new stage of my life.

Even when I knew I was in the grip of the darkest storm and I needed help again, I didn't want to go back to medication or immerse myself in eternal therapy.

I wanted to make radical, meaningful, beneficial, permanent changes.

I visited eight specialists, including psychologists and psychiatrists. When in the second or third consultation they tried to medicate me, I ran away.

After many turns, someone recommended me a holistic psychologist. With her, the therapies were advancing along paths unknown to me until then. She applied methods that allowed me to push a lot of repressed emotions out, very ugly and old emotions that were hurting me.

One of the therapies, for example, consisted of me sitting down every day for three minutes to complain. At first, it was easy:

"My life sucks. I'm not capable of anything. I don't have a successful job. I'm getting old, and I haven't married. I haven't seen my parents for a long time. I'm not successful. I am not prosperous. I was never able to practice dentistry."

There came a time when I felt so fed up with my own complaints that I realized this descent into the worst part of myself disgusted me. I thought I shouldn't complain so much.

Another therapy was to write down each day five things for which I was grateful. At first, I wrote down lofty events: the air, the sunrise, breathing. Gradually, I became more and more appreciative of simple things that made the right and left hemispheres of my brain work at the same time. I had never done that before. I began to level out, to feel better.

One day that psychologist asked me:

"How about starting meditation?"

At that point, everything changed.

That was a one-hundred-and-eighty-degree turn in my life, but this time for good and, above all, for the better.

WHEN THE LIPS ARE SILENT,
THE HEART HAS A HUNDRED TONGUES

1.

"Meditate? That's not for me," was my automatic response.

The psychologist introduced me to a war veteran, a patient of hers, and he joined the conversation:

"Meditation's going to change your life; it changed mine."

The insistence and the signs were so many that I sought a meditation center.

The first day, I was totally lost. I couldn't concentrate, let alone get rid of thoughts and obsessions. I'd open my eyes and wonder how all those people could be sitting there so peacefully. I'd look at the watch—time did not pass. I opened and closed my eyes again. I was almost overflowing with restlessness. I repeated to myself it was not for me; stillness is a word that was not part of my days.

A few sessions later, when I understood what anchoring the breath meant, I began to feel the benefits of meditating. It was about refocusing on the breathing every time my mind wandered somewhere else, every time I was plagued by thoughts. I understood there's no such thing as a blank mind, only letting thoughts pass.

I began to feel better. People around me noticed it. When they asked me what I was doing, and I answered I was meditating, they gave me funny looks, in disbelief, because of the limited knowledge they had about the practice. However, I made my family and many friends approach meditation, and quite a few of them continued practicing it. I sent them videos and audio files. It was my new life, and I wanted to share it.

2.

As always, my scientific spirit and my natural restlessness prevailed, and I felt the need to go a step further. To go deeper, to investigate, to acquire knowledge.

Thus began a path whose end is still far away.

I bought many books; I read everything I could.

One day I said to myself, "If this interests you so much, you have to study it with a formal approach, one that allows you to help other people."

It was 2020; I was beginning my covid-19 lockup, and the best way I found to take advantage of the circumstances was to take an online course. It took over four hundred hours; I put all my time and passion into it. I was finally coming to understand what was going on with my body and brain while meditating; neuroscience was yielding the answers. It was like opening portals of knowledge that placed me in the roots and history of everything I was learning. It was universal knowledge, as ancient as it was contemporary, capable of providing answers to people of any age, social status, and religious beliefs.

I thought meditation and yoga went hand in hand. I was also very interested in meditation in movement. Then I took a two-hundred-hour course—at an institute in Madrid, also online—of Hatha Vinyasa Yoga, one of the most widespread yoga disciplines in the world, focused on asanas or postures, which require concentration and calm.

I was piling hours of flight for myself and then transmitting them to others, which is my most genuine interest and my path to solidarity and empathy.

3.

Connecting from Minneapolis, Minnesota, I took many of the courses; I had gone there to spend some time.

My then partner lived there. He was a delightful American man whom I had met through a friend. We had a beautiful relationship, full of peace, unlike any other I had experienced. Although that relationship ended and had its mourning, it didn't lead me to depression. I had the tools to face the situation, to avoid victimizing myself, and to assume with mental clarity my failures and even the things I couldn't control. I had the emotional intelligence to withdraw when I saw this relationship wasn't going where I wanted it to go, which was to create a home and reach a state of loving stability and peace. I learned a lot from that love and especially from that ex-partner because he's a chiropractor, and he understood the whole process I was going through; we shared it. He was a great teacher in that particular moment of my life.

At that time, living with a partner didn't mean a radical change but a way of being in the present, of accessing an opportunity for emotional and spiritual growth.

The present in Miami was confinement. In addition, I was out of work. In Minnesota, on the other hand, the circumstances with covid-19 seemed less dramatic; everything was open and relatively normal.

I remember one of our first outings in Minnesota was to Norman County, in the northern part of the state. We climbed a small mountain. I have no words to describe the beauty of that autumn landscape, with green, yellow, red, and orange trees. I had never been so moved by a landscape.

I cried. For the first time, I cried at the joy, the fullness, the gratitude, the beauty.

4.

While still in Minnesota, I started posting some meditation tips on my Instagram account and sharing how I was feeling. I very timidly offered meditation classes. I thought I was ready to guide a meditator's first steps, even though I was still studying and learning.

From such an informal beginning grew something that became, more than a job, a life project. I came to help two hundred and fifty people online. I could see that most of them were going through a process of depression, and I wasn't a psychologist; I could only guide them to seek professional help and take the best from meditation. They were going through the natural consequences of confinement, difficult family life, and also a lot of loneliness.

I myself was suffering from the aftereffects of those complex months. Although I felt fine, I noticed an unnatural weariness; it was hard for me to concentrate; harder than what's normal for me.

I had blood tests to determine how my values were. These tests showed results I'd never have imagined.

On the one hand, the levels of mercury in my blood were high because I had been a pescatarian for ten years, that is, eating only vegetables and fish, especially tuna. And we already know that mercury can be very toxic to the immune and nervous systems and many organs. I was forced to eat meat again, but always in moderation.

On the other hand, the analysis of vitamins and other elements indicated that I had vitamin B deficiencies and very low serotonin.

I had blamed external factors—even my heredity— for all my problems when many of them were in my own blood. The imbalance of serotonin, a neurotransmitter known as the hormone of happiness, explained much of my melancholy, uncontrollable sadness, eventual lack of appetite, listlessness, pessimism, and insomnia. Depression and lack of self-esteem could also be directly associated with serotonin, a mood regulator.

It's incredible to me that none of the psychologists and psychiatrists I went to for so many years ever thought of asking for blood tests, considering how simple it is to increase serotonin levels: through foods rich in tryptophan and with activities as rewarding as meditation, yoga, exercise, a hug, living in a state of gratitude.

From then on, changing my diet and taking vitamin supplements, along with meditation and yoga, made me feel much better, and that, in turn, opened the floodgates to the need to know how my body worked in relation to my mind, to look for scientific explanations of that relationship.

That's how I came to the book *The Molecule of More* by Daniel Z. Lieberman and Michael E. Long. The former is a renowned psychiatrist, and the latter is a physicist by training and a writer. The book, in a nutshell, explained to me the role of dopamine in the history of human behavior and how dopaminergic circuits, although they're what makes us create, imagine and dream, can't be the only way to find harmony, which is the goal of a fulfilling, happy life.

As the authors point out, dopamine is a molecule that generates addiction but at the same time, perpetual dissatisfaction. Neurotransmitters, or "here-and-now molecules," include serotonin, oxytocin, endorphins, and endocannabinoids, which, unlike dopamine, give us pleasure from sensations and emotions: "If we're able to combine dopamine with here-and-now neurotransmitters, we can achieve that harmony. But the constant craving for dopamine is not a path to the best possible future; it is the combined work of sensory reality and abstract thinking that unleashes the full potential of the brain. If it works optimally, it's capable of generating not only happiness and satisfaction, not only wealth and knowledge but also a rich mixture of sensory experience and wise knowledge, a mixture that can lead us to a more balanced way of being human," say Lieberman and Long.

There must be a balance between spirituality and the knowledge that comes from science. This contributes to a fuller and more open life, open to empathy. Meditation has scientifically proven benefits and is not linked to any religious belief, dogma, or paradigm.

Although meditation has its origins in Eastern religions, almost all the world's religions, in one way or another, promote the principles of meditation, whether through contemplation, prayer, chanting, or confession. It's that moment when you break your routine and, in full attention, dedicate yourself to an activity and concentrate on it, whatever the purpose is. Everything comes to a standstill to fulfill that.

Meditating is not holding our thoughts; it's observing them with a gentle curiosity. What we seek when we meditate is a state of attention focused on a thought, a feeling, an object, a concentration, the perception of the senses. When we achieve this, we create the "present moment."

5.

The blood tests revealed another great reality: my fertile life is conditioned by a hormone no gynecologist had ever told me about. The so-called anti-mullerian hormone is in charge of the number of eggs a woman has during her reproductive life, and many of us don't know that number decreases as we get older. If you're a woman reading this and are in your thirties or older, I invite you to talk to your doctor about this hormone.

It was not easy for me to come to terms with this.

It was a setback out of my control, threatening what I had been dreaming of for so long—a family.

When I turned thirty-five, I made the decision to preserve my eggs. I did it serenely, without ethical regrets, accepting that it was my present and my reality. If science offers us an honest hand, we must humbly accept. I believe credibility is forged not by pretending to be perfect but by being honest.

I know I want to have a child, and I can't guess when the right person will come along to start a family, if ever. My eggs are in safekeeping. It's one of the ways I have to control some of my future. You have to do everything you can to build the future you want.

6.

To go even deeper into mindfulness and meditation, I went to learn directly from people I regard as models in the field, people I admire and follow very closely.

I had listened to the TED talk *The Power of Mindfulness* by Shauna Shapiro, a clinical psychologist and specialist in mindfulness and compassion. Then I looked up her book *Good Morning, I Love You: Mindfulness and Self-Compassion Practices to Rewire Your Brain for Calm, Clarity and Joy*. When I finished reading it, I wrote a post on my Instagram account and received thanks from the foundation she leads; then she herself wrote me, sent me a book, and invited me to participate in a retreat at the Esalen Institute in Big Sur, California.

It was my first total disconnection retreat. There was no television, no internet, no phone signal. That disconnection reconnected me with myself. It was an unforgettable experience, one that I talk about every chance I get.

I learned a lot from Shauna Shapiro; I was initially seduced by the fact that she, a bit like me, had come to meditation in the most turbulent time of her life.

That ten-day retreat, set in a spectacular oceanfront mountain location, was perfect for me to connect with nature and assimilate Shapiro's teachings that the brain can rewire itself to bring us deep calm, clarity, and joy. It was exactly what I was looking for myself and to pass on to others through my project.

Before going to Esalen, I had read *The Molecule of More*, and what it says about how addicted we are to dopamine began to make sense as I related it to Shapiro's proposal that mindfulness, instead of trying to control or judge our experience, is about putting interest in it with attitudes of compassion and openness, recognizing a human dimension of absolute awareness. She says, and I share it: "We all have the capacity to change. Science proves it. No matter what your past is, no matter what your current circumstances are, it's never too late to rewire your brain for greater calm, clarity, and joy."

Later on, I did a yoga retreat in the Bahamas, then two more in Colorado with Joe Dispenza, a chiropractor by profession, writer, and lecturer specializing in neurology, neuroscience, and biochemistry. With him, I experienced other types of meditation, more focused on relaxation and deeper concentration, using sounds. He points out that our minds and thoughts can transform reality. Many elements of his philosophy were very familiar to me and still had links to my interest in neurotransmitters: "The scan of someone with anxiety or depression is the same: the brain starts to secrete chemistry as if what the person fears is happening, and over time that chemistry becomes addictive."

It was a journey, as Despenza says, "into a quantum field" of unlimited energy, the one leading to the transformation of our reality.

"There is a synchronization between your energy and your future, and the side effect of that is the signals." I was picking up all the signals and transforming my emotions for the better.

"You have to stop thinking about the predictable future and the familiar past, go straight to the present moment, and go from being some time to being no time." I was, as I had never been, in the here and now.

At the same time, I took courses in Bhakti Yoga, which focuses on loving devotion and isn't only practiced in stillness.

I also went to a Vipassana retreat in Baja California. I had been preparing myself for that experience: ten days in absolute silence, long meditations, getting up early, no communication of any kind with the outside world, no talking to anyone in the group, with my eyes always lowered. It reminded me of my days in Jerusalem. Maybe that's why I was able to endure. Quite a few people give up in the first few days. I cried the first and second days; I thought I couldn't go on, then I gave in to the experience.

It all came together.

As I shape this book, I am completing a second certification in Vinyasa Yoga 200 YTT (two hundred hours of Yoga Teacher Training in the Ahana Style stream) and another in Jivamukti Yoga 75 YTT (seventy-five hours of Yoga Teacher Training in the Jivamukti Yoga style). This will lead me to offer yoga training as a teacher.

I plan to keep growing, discovering, and never stop being a student of life because I'm deeply passionate about it.

For the time being, I have no dramatic conclusions. I own no truths or concrete phrases to explain the way forward.

I'm not the owner of any truth. I'm getting closer to the degree of consciousness I was looking for; I'm resolving my dealings with the past, with painful relationships, with the Vanessa who suffered and invested so much in longings that weren't fulfilled. But there is still a long way to go, and for now, I'm grateful for everything I'm learning.

I don't know anything about the future either.

"Sing your own song of happiness the way you choose to sing it, without worrying or caring what it's supposed to be like," recommends Wayne Dyer.

I'm in a place of more calm and peace than I've ever been in my life. I'm singing my happiness as I can, in my own way; I am in the present tense. I'm sure that everything I've lived through has been to get to this moment, this place, these pages. Everything reiterates to me what, for some years now, have been basic rules in my life which I seek to repeat to myself daily:

1) Make love the unifier of your life, guiding all your motives, decisions and actions.

2) Take time once a day to be grateful.

3) Take time to enjoy life: laugh a lot.

4) Do more of the things you love and less of the things that kill your spirit.

5) Surround yourself with people who inspire you.

6) You may never be the best in the world, but you can always do your best.

7) Have sincere motives toward others.

8) Accept the future as an adventure.

9) Keep your integrity with boundaries and your imagination without limits.

10) Don't be afraid to be vulnerable.

Miami, August 2022

Sentences That Led the Way

The phrases that title each chapter have inspired me in many different ways, and they have come to me through very diverse paths I'm grateful for: through readings, friends, chance.

"The beauty of cracks" comes from a chapter in the book *The Power of Being Vulnerable*, by Brené Brown; "A Portuguese home with certainty is certainly a Portuguese home" is part of a verse from a beautiful fado by Amalia Rodrigues; "Barefoot I come, from the far reaches of childhood" is from another fado by Amalia Rodrigues; "My life is reborn in this wounded corner of mine" comes from a poem by Ricardo Ribeiro; "Beauty is the name of something that doesn't exist" is from the Portuguese poet Fernando Pessoa; "Tristeza não tem fim, felicidade sim" is from the song by Tom Jobim and Vinicius De Moraes; "For strong as death is love" is a from a passage from the Song of Songs, from the Old Testament; "And she heard the voice of God in a blind well" comes also from a verse by Fernando Pessoa; "With the lust of darkness" is part of a poem by the Portuguese writer Nuno Júdice; and finally, "When the lips are silent, the heart has a hundred tongues" is a phrase from the Persian mystic poet Rumi.

Made in the USA
Columbia, SC
04 August 2023

21291799R00115